# THOSE FLEETING YEARS

*by* Luba Czerhoniak Fedash

**DORRANCE**
PUBLISHING CO
EST. 1920
PITTSBURGH, PENNSYLVANIA 15222

Dorrance Publishing Co., Inc.
701 Smithfield Street
Pittsburgh, PA 15222
Visit our website at www.dorrancebookstore.com

ISBN: 978-1-4809-0194-0
eISBN: 978-1-4809-0464-0

# Dedication

To my dearly beloved, late husband of forty-eight years, John; to my pride and joy daughters, Kyra and Laura, and their loving families; to the "Lemko" people everywhere.

# Acknowledgment

A special "thank you" to my most caring daughters, Kyra and Laura, and their precious families for encouraging me to write this narrative—*Those Fleeting Years*—a sequel to *Blossoms On a Rooftop*.

# Contents

# Reflections on *Those Fleeting Years*

"To everything there is a season, and a time to every purpose under heaven: A time to be born, and a time to die; a time to plant, and a time to pluck up that which is planted: A time to weep, and a time to laugh; a time to mourn, and a time to dance," Ecclesiastes 3 (KJV).

Like birds on a wing, seasons come and seasons go, each in its own time and for its own purpose. Let's start with the season which follows winter—the wondrous season of spring—when new cycles of life for all hibernating living things begin over again. Spring! That magical time of year, when Mother Nature transforms the endless fields of monotonous snows to endless fields of shimmering, emerald-green grasses intermingled with profusion of radiant wild flowers under the sunny blue skies, gentle sweeping breezes and just enough rain to keep the healthy growth propagating; when trees of all sizes and shapes—ravaged by winter storms to the point of lifelessness to the eye of the beholder—burst forth with new leaves and blooms; when our singing feathered friends return from their wintering locations and begin scrambling for safe nesting places for their young to be; when humble dandelions invade our front lawns, and more respected and appreciated perfumed hyacinths, purple violets, yellow daffodils, and colorful tulips dazzle the world around us with their enchanting beauty. Spring is that intoxicating time of year—as well as of our lives—we wish could last forever. But nothing ever does—good or not so good—in nature or in life. On the heels of spring is summer.

The magic of summer can be seen in a child's happy face safe in loved one's arms, jumping over the roaring ocean waves; in the eyes of a little boy or girl digging in the warm sand, or collecting shells washed upon the shore, marveling at the wonder of it all; in the flight of a beautiful monarch butterfly or a tiny humming bird flitting from one nectar-enhanced bush to another; in the sight of ripe, plump, red cherries, strawberries and raspberries, which were delicate pink and white flowers our eyes feasted upon—what seems like only yesterday—last spring. Too soon the long sunny days of summer—when the living is easy and at the peak of our enjoyment—must bid us good-bye, because the season of autumn is waiting for her turn on nature's stage.

With summer gone, autumn is now showcasing its wonders; apple trees laden with red, green, and yellow juicy fruit; pear trees with nectar-sweet pears, vegetables and grains ready for harvesting. And, of course, oodles of the impressive in size and color pumpkins ready for picking in the fields and on the roadside stands—the highlight of the fall season, and delight to people of all ages, but especially the children. The season of autumn, on some level, could appropriately be compared to a "Midas touch" in remembrance of a legendary ancient king who was given the power of turning everything he touched to gold, as does Mother Nature in autumn: changing the green fields to golden ones, green leaves to shining color of gold, and the white, full summer moon to an autumn golden one as well. At the end of this golden season, we take a break from our labor (the fourth Thursday in November) in commemoration of the first Thanksgiving celebrated by one of the English colonists settling in Plymouth in 1620, for the purpose of giving thanks to God for His divine goodness. Anytime after Thanksgiving, we can expect the season of winter to arrive on the scene with His gifts of marvels.

Often unexpectedly, Mother Nature—with Father Frost's help—drops a blanket of white fluff from Her domain in the sky, changing our surroundings of golden fields to a land of tranquil white the winter wonderland artists love to paint, skiers delight to ski upon, and the rest of us simply choose to enjoy—or tolerate—while secretly wishing for spring and long sunny days of summer to return.

The cycle of seasons is now complete which translates to one year in our busy lives. But it all happened so quickly, we muse, and for a good reason. It really did! "One season following another laden with happiness and tears." (A passage from *Fiddler on a Roof*). *One* year stealthily turning to another, and then into history and eternity.

Watching from atop a hill and enjoying the merriment of unfamiliar children's faces and voices, the bespectacled elderly woman reminisced about her own moments of childhood joy upon a similar slope in another place—far away and long ago—also covered by a blanket of white fluff. But in a blink of an eye, or so it seemed to her in retrospect, the white fluff upon which she was standing abruptly changed to a blanket of lush green spring grass. To her amazement—and just as abruptly—the entire scene in her mind changed to a bright, sunny summer day, reminiscent of her long gone youth. Bewildered, she found herself looking over a picturesque scene of rolling hills and valleys covered by falling red and gold autumn leaves, also reminiscent of her much younger days. Perplexed, she checked to see if her booted feet were still firmly planted on the same snowy hill where the children were playing. Everything seemed to check out perfectly, including the reality of the rapidity of the seasons and years that so swiftly passed her by nearly unnoticeably. Where have all the decades gone? Almost eight of them! She questioned the snowy surroundings around her on a windy hill. Finally, the universal truth hit home! Time is a fleeting, precious commodity we are blessed with for a specific reason, and only one lifetime per individual—however long or short that may be—to be enjoyed, and none of it to be wasted.

# Chapter One
## The Days Don't Know
## What the Years Will Bring

The days of our lives are measured by the orbits (revolutions) of the planet Earth around the luminous celestial body the sun, from which we receive heat and light necessary for life on earth as we know it. Simple and clear, right? Not really! Not to a six or seven-year-old child watching over the family's three dairy cows, day in and day out—except for the winter months—rain or shine, from sunrise to sunset, far away from home and alone.

There were only two constants in this child's young life: the sunrise and the sunset. Sunrise, when she freed the herd from their stalls in the barn, guided them to the pasture fields in the forest clearing a mile or so away from her home, where they grazed all day while she watched so they didn't wander from their designated grazing areas and encroached upon the family's or neighbors' precious growing plants, the struggling villagers, ravaged by evil Hitler's Second World War, depended on for their winter sustenance. Wheat, barley, oats, potatoes, cabbage, turnips, beets and carrots—these were the staple crops of the poor farmers' customary diet, especially the potatoes and sauerkraut (cabbage cut fine and fermented in a brine made of its own juice and salt).

Sunset, when the little girl knew it was time to bring the herd back to their stalls in the barn, wake up with the sun the next morning, and start the routine over again. And that was all the child knew—and needed to know—about the sun, which she at times chastised for moving too fast through the sky on bright, warm days she was enjoying with her natural family in the forest of tall trees, singing birds, wild flowers, and babbling brooks. And too slow on cold rainy days, when she was drenched to the bone and wished she was at home close to her human family she shared her love with and was a part of.

Often, the little girl's eyes would become fixated on the great orange ball in the sky where God and His angels live, as her mother had taught her. But as hard as she prayed to get at least a glimpse of the bearded, very old man she imagined God to be and the beautiful flying angels around Him, her prayers remained unanswered. The little shepherdess was too young to understand that God was right there with her at all times. He was there when her small, emaciated, tuberculosis-ridden body was ready to let go of its spirit, but miraculously became healed without medical intervention—only her mother's fervent prayers and the whispering healing pine trees, fresh mountain air, and pure spring water where she spent her days watching over the family's herd. He was there when the bombs fell so close to the pasture fields where the child—with her herd—happened to be at the time, and the impact caused her, along with the cattle, to pass out for an indefinite period until her frightened-to-death mother found her seemingly lifeless body and, by the grace of God, brought her back to life, but not without scars, such as a partial destruction of the retina in the right eye which compromised her vision and nerve endings in the left ear, which caused a permanent loss of hearing. He was there when a big, grey wolf approached the young shepherdess and threatened to attack but changed his mind and walked away. Thankfully, it was wolf and not the evil Hitler himself, or one of his puppets without human conscience, because the wild beast walked away without harming the little girl or the cattle in her care, and Hitler and his kind might not have if their wicked spirit moved them to inflict harm on the innocent.

This was war at its worst! Most everything the poor mountain-folk raised on their rocky, hilly land belonged to Hitler's regime, as well as anything else that fancied their whim—like the family's one and only dearly loved horse named Chestnut which was taken from them—because they were under Hitler's occupation, and refusing, or even questioning, anything the Nazi Gestapo wanted was like asking for fate worse than death. Hunger was the norm for all six years of the Second World War. But hunger alone does not always begin and end with lack of food. Emotional hunger can be equally as devastating and destroying as the physical one. Hitler's disregard for the human spirit, dignity, and life itself of those unfortunates who were different from him and his chosen ones, by virtue of looks and beliefs, was a spiritual starvation and suffocation from the get go. How sad that a child of six or seven had to assume the responsibility of an adult, be taught to keep secrets at all cost, and lie for self-preservation and those she loved.

The little girl was not even nine when another dreadful responsibility fell upon her small shoulders. This time, to keep watch for the Nazi soldiers arriving in the village on horseback in search of able-bodied young men and women—like her eighteen-year-old brother, Michael—hiding in a space created for him by his loved ones beneath the floor of the family's log home, to avoid being forcibly taken by Gestapo to God only knew where. The youngster was instructed by her mother, Tekla, and fifteen-year-old brother, John—now responsible for his little sister's job of herding the livestock to the pastures and helping his mother in raising of crops—to be very vigilant in her responsibility because the family's lives depended on how fast she could run through the village to check on Nazi presence, and presume innocence when confronted with the swastika-soldiers. Thankfully, she always managed to hide her brother before the Nazi reached her home and successfully convinced them each time she knew nothing about Michael's whereabouts. But the day of reckoning caught up with Michael and his family. On the way to find another hiding place, he was apprehended on a train and taken to Auschwitz concentration camp where he spent two tormenting years, until his liberation at the end of that horrendous World War II when Hitler, the self-named fuehrer, was defeated.

The young shepherdess described above is me—Luba—the author of *Those Fleeting Years,* a sequel to *Blossoms on a Rooftop,* published by Dorrance Publishing Company in Pittsburgh,

Pennsylvania in 2006, which is still available through them as well as Amazon.com and some bookstores.

My wish in this chapter is to build a plausible footbridge connecting *Blossoms on a Rooftop* to its sequel, *Those Fleeting Years,* to make it easier for the reader to visualize my story in its entirety through *Those Fleeting Years* alone.

I was born on May 10, 1933 in southeast corner of present-day Poland in the Carpathian Mountains known as the Lemko region or Lemkovyna. My childhood was short-lived, interrupted first by the chatter of the approaching Second World War, followed by Hitler's attack on Poland and his occupation in 1939, including the mountainous Lemko region, where, as a very young shepherdess, I thought I belonged and would spend the rest of my life in my ancestral log home on the land my enigmatic father in America inherited from his parents, and they—retrospectively—from theirs, and so on…through generations. This was my forever home and my destiny; I presumptuously assumed, failing to acknowledge one fundamental fact of life I recognize today as the truth: The days don't know what the years will bring—the title of this chapter.

I turned fourteen in May of 1947, and in July of that year—out of nowhere—armed soldiers appeared at our doorstep and seemingly guiltlessly, boldly declared: "You have two hours to pack your belongings and be ready to leave your home, along with your livestock." And leave we did without knowing the reason, if there was one, for this absurdity, but out of fear, and some screwy law that was hanging over our confused heads, with hardly a spare minute to say a brief good-bye to our ancestral log home and everything our ancestors and we worked for up to that dreadful moment. For me personally, this act of injustice was beyond my comprehension. Was this for real or a bad dream I would soon wake up from? But there was no waking up for me and for us as a family. In a matter of hours, we found ourselves homeless, squeezed into a windowless box car of a transport train, sharing the space with our three cows which appeared as confused as we were. Not only were we homeless, we didn't know where we were being shipped to or what we would find there.

Three weeks (plus) of an arduous journey, we found ourselves in a strange land in the southwestern part of Poland known as Silesia, which was the home to the German people before the war. That was where we were forced to resettle, along with other Lemko families from other villages, but none from ours. The families from "Leszczyny" (our village) were dropped off in other locations of Silesia. To add insult to injury, we were forbidden to return, or even visit our own homeland in the Carpathian Mountains for many years to come. Grudgingly, I made up my mind to accept what could not be changed. Encouraged by my mother, I decided I might as well put all my efforts into an education, which eluded me during my formative years back home in my Lemkovyna due to the war. My education at age fourteen was equivalent to second grade at best, and it was in my native Cyrillic alphabet and the Lemko dialect, closely related to Ukrainian and other Slavic languages. Surprisingly, I realized almost an instantaneous success in fifth grade where I was placed since this was the highest grade in the village school. I skipped the sixth grade altogether, and became an honor student in the seventh grade about twelve kilometers from home in the city of Glogow where I boarded with a local family during the snowy winter months, and commuted the rest of time via a dilapidated bicycle one of my brothers put together for himself from found parts in the war ruins. Becoming fluent in Polish—without a trace of an accent—would have helped me to move on in school…to the heights of my scholastic ability and desire; unfortunately, not as a Lemko or Ukrainian as we were referred to by people who didn't know our history and why suddenly we appeared on their land. Once again, this was not to be, because my destiny was elsewhere—in another part of the world and another foreign land.

Coming home from school for the weekend some time in March of 1949, another unthinkable and unexpected event dared to face me. "Luba, your father in America wrote this letter to you," my mother said as she handed me an open envelope which contained a lengthy letter to her and a brief note to me, certainly not meriting another life-changing situation I was about to face.

> *"My dear daughter, it is my sincere wish that you*
> *join me in America and continue your education*
> *here, now that the war is finally over and I am able*
> *to bring you, and only you, since you are still a*

*minor and I am an American citizen and had been at*
*the time of your birth."*
         Signed—*Your Loving Father in America*

I read the note several times over to make some sense of this short note, but failed. I stuffed it back in the envelope and returned it to Mother, feeling assured she would not agree to that absurd request/demand, especially since I didn't really know my father and was doing so well in school. Wrong!

"Luba, your father cut through a lot of red tape to get to this point and you cannot disappoint him."

Did I hear right? Was I being forced out from this home too! No amount of pleading would change my mother's made-up mind. She insisted my father knew best, and she agreed that emigrating to America to live with him was the right thing for my future, even though it didn't include her and my two dear brothers. My parents' decision was final and Michael and John cast their vote to their side, to my utter disappointment. "Luba, you must go!" They both mimicked my mother's decision. Once again, the previous day of my life did not know what the next day was about to spring on me.

I arrived in America on May 14, 1949—four days after my sixteenth birthday. The difficulties I encountered, at first, seemed insurmountable. Fortunately, my determination, willingness to work hard, perseverance, and desire to please my father all worked in my favor and my father's pride.

The strange land and an enigmatic father I once feared materialized to two prominent positives in my life. I not only eventually fell in love with my adopted country of America, but also learned to love my father unconditionally and as much as I loved my dear mother and brothers back home.

One moment in time which stands above many other memorable ones in my life on this side of the ocean, was the day I became a bona fide American citizen at the ripe young age of twenty-one. Finally, I had a country to proudly call my own. My America! My forever home, sweet home!

# Chapter Two
# English as a Second Language (For Me)

Something to do, somebody to love, something to look forward to are—no doubt—ingredients necessary for a happy, rewarding, and fulfilling life. To this list of basic fundamentals in this group, I would like to add one more ingredient—**challenge!** Without challenges life would be a mere ordinary existence, lacking excitement, sense of accomplishment, interest, satisfaction, and overall wellbeing. Challenges always worked for me if I knew what they were. But in the case of analogies, metaphors, clichés, and particularities inherent to conversational English, such essentials did not extend to my vocabulary in the initial years of my learning English as a second language, simply because their importance was not stressed enough in school or particularly required in the technically oriented working world.

As a secretary in an engineering department of a prominent telephone company of the time—Western Electric—I handled my multitask responsibilities with ease and felt comfortable in my—well-respected—position on all levels. I felt gratified that my hard work in pursuit of proper English was finally bearing fruit of sweet success. I had learned everything there was to learn and now it was time to collect well-deserved rewards—I dared to think. *Not so fast!* A gentle voice in my head interrupted and warned. *If you want to collect rewards you must continue on learning. Learning is a lifelong occupation. And heaven only knows how many more lifetimes of living you might need if you stop learning now, yet expect blessings of rewards to go on. Life is not that simple! You must earn your rewards through continuous learning.* Was this my conscience reminding me of this universal truth? Whatever it was, it was real and spoke honestly, loud and clear. I needed to hear this and take it all in, before my fallacious thinking about education had a chance to root itself into my mind and further confuse me. Fortunately, that didn't come to pass. It took but one trip to a men's sporting goods department store to make me realize how much more there was to this complex English language waiting for me to discover and make it my own.

It is in my nature to take life's challenges very seriously. And it was on this Saturday morning on a shopping trip to buy something new for myself and an item my brother John—in the old country—had been asking me for, that I faced a challenge which left me mortified and made me realize how much more there was to this colorful English language that would continue to challenge my fluency.

"I would like to purchase a pair of **horse pants** for my brother." I heard myself sputter confidently to the salesman in the men's sporting department. It sounded just fine to me without the adjective "riding" (horse-riding pants).

"And what size is your horse, pray tell?" The sales man asked loud enough for the question to carry throughout the small store, which resulted in snickers and laughter—obviously at my expense. I stormed out of the place, barely holding back tears until I closed the door behind me. On the way home—without any purchases—the voice in my head made itself known again. *If you think this was embarrassing, imagine yourself in a social situation where you want to impress someone special, but you don't understand the meaning of the various clichés used in the conversation.* And again, the message was loud and clear and to the point. It was true, I hardly ever paid attention to unique American culture expressions, because to me, they sounded strange, insensitive and—most of all—because I didn't understand the hidden meanings behind them....

In retrospect, the embarrassing experience in the men's sporting department that day turned out to be a blessing in disguise, because it was that defining moment that made me see how important new phrases, expressions, analogies, unusual words, and such were to conversational English. I became fascinated and challenged by them, and eager to impress special people in my life through their proper usage. Literally, I went after them much like a "bull in a china closet." As strange as this comparison may seem, I feel completely justified in using it.

In time, I forgave the person who skinned the cat, because I knew no animal was actually hurt. This metaphorical or analogous phrase simply denoted an overzealous individual who left "no stones unturned" in pursuit of specific goals, thus the strange expression "there are many ways to skin a cat." By the same token, "mudslinging" did not depict real mud fights, similar to ones I remembered from my native Carpathian Mountains between children looking for excitement in otherwise mundane environment. It simply meant unfavorable things uncovered about a political opponent and used against him/her in campaigns.

"Stay out of the kitchen if you can't stand the heat." Didn't mean you could no longer enjoy a home-cooked meal because you were unable to cook in a hot kitchen. Rather, it meant: don't get involved in something you can't handle. Well put!

"Don't upset the apple cart." Didn't mean to be careful not to overturn the cart because the apples will fall out of it. Unraveled, it meant: be peaceful. Don't look for trouble where there is none. If things are going well, leave them alone. If something is not broken, don't try to fix it.

"If life gives you lemons make lemonade." Didn't mean you were doomed to squeezing lemons for the rest of your life. Simply put, it meant: we can't always control what happens to us in life, but we can control how we deal with it. I could go on and on…but I know, "you get my drift." I have no intention here—or anywhere else—to "beat the horse to death." I am an animal lover and the phrase alone brings tears to my eyes, even though the expression merely means don't dwell on something forever…move on. But I do feel compelled to share my most recent episode in hopes that it will amuse you as much as it amused me after the fact.

On a recent one-day excursion to Atlantic City, a friend wished me to "break a leg." I was highly insulted by her insensitive remark, since I had not heard the phrase before and actually thought she wished me bad luck, which would follow me until her foreboding was fulfilled. While on the boardwalk in Atlantic City, I sat on a bench for most of the sunny summer afternoon for fear of really breaking one or both of my legs, instead of taking a delightful walk by the rippling ocean waves I was so looking forward to, have a memorable meal, and do a little gambling before returning home at the end of the day. Days later, I confessed my continued fear of an impending misfortune to a compassionate neighbor who assured me no such incident was about to befall me or anytime in the future, because my friend sincerely wished me "good luck" by that unusual expression. What a waste of a beautiful day to my later regret!

I give you permission to have a chuckle on me when you come across a unique expression—one inherent to the English language alone—and imagine what my initial perception of its literal interpretation might have been, before "the light bulb went on in my head," and graced my world with enough brightness to see deeper into the "grassroots" of this colorful language—called English—I proudly adopted for my own. I feel blessed to be a witness to its ever-changing, growing vocabulary, phraseology, analogies, metaphors, and clichés, and intend to keep up with them, because I learned over the years that life is one continuous learning journey, no matter where our destiny may lead us or how long we live. And may we never forget that once we stop learning, we stop living.

# Chapter Three
# Those Were the Days (of My Youth)

"Youth is wasted on the young," I heard some people say. I respect-fully disagree. Youth is the indispensable part of every person's "rite of passage." In the long run and larger scheme of things, it is the youth of today who are destined to inherit the leadership of tomorrow's world. In view of the rapidly changing socioeconomic conditions in our shrinking global world of today— coupled with fierce competition —the young, presently under our guardianship, must be adequately educated not only in the fields of speedily expending and progressing technologies, but also in the psychologies of different people's cul-tures, to better understand them in order to attain peace and harmony in the world of today as well as the future.

I would feel remiss if I didn't quote at this opportune moment a passage from one of the most beloved authors of the time, Bess Streeter Aldrich's timeless classic, *A White Bird Flying,* (Copyright, 1931, by D. Appleton and Company), which left a lasting impression not only on my own youth but my life as well.

>    **"Youth** sees life as a plot, a happy, romantic adventuresome plot. But they who have lived past their youthfulness, know that life does not arrange

itself forever in well-defined patterns, nor does it always arrive at solutions. Life is like a river—a groping, pulsing river, endlessly rising and falling, finding its way through mists and shadows to some far sea. Every human is a part of the interminable flow. Every human is a part of the story. One life touches another and is gone. There is contact for a brief time—an influence for good or ill. And the river goes on, endlessly rising and falling, finding its way to the sea."

Let me, at this time, bring to light two golden rules I have learned early on in life, still live by today, and believe would serve well the present generation of young people awaiting their turn on the world stage of leaders. And they are: "Live and let live" and "Do unto others as you would want them do unto you." Two simple but powerful universal truths—a tribute to the essence of things past, present, and future. If we leave to them—the leaders of tomorrow in training today—the best of ourselves through good examples, we would have left them a recipe for a joyous and successful life. And a legacy they could proudly bequeath to their children in waiting and so on…into perpetuity.

Youth is the time for the young to grow and bloom. A time to spread their fledgling wings and soar to the heights equal to their strengths, desires, and abilities; a time for discoveries of their attributes and weaknesses and build upon them; a time to bathe in their youthfulness and experience the best life has to offer through undaunted diligence, responsibility, loyalty, and respect for themselves and others.

My own youth of the '30s, '40s, the fabulous '50s, and the '60s encompassed many different stages and phases. Some filled with sadness and loneliness, some astoundingly happy, some status quo, all natural for the time in history and my life. The '30s and the '40s reflect the events of the Second World War under Hitler's occupation which harbored an uncanny fear, uncertainty, complete mistrust, and danger at every turn. Fortunately—and out of necessity—I became a true lover of nature very early in life which sustained me through the war years and beyond, and blessed me with a strong will to live and spirit to keep on regenerating my strength during the most trying time of my childhood, when the war was raging around us. Nature brought joy to my otherwise mundane day-to-day life in the fields, watching over the cattle. But I desperately feared the snakes—and I still do today— which encroached on my joy of nature.

I concur, snakes deserve to live, hopefully in harmony with other ground-bound creatures, but I don't want them slithering in my path. My apologies to the serpent-enthusiasts. Furthermore, just because I am afraid of snakes as a result of one unpleasant and frightening encounter with a snake while picking mushrooms as a youngster in a different part of the world, doesn't mean anybody else should harbor the same fear. So, enjoy your passion for snakes, if that happens to be your fervor. Somebody has to look out for those slipping creatures too. Pardon me, but it can't be me. Enough rambling about my fear of snakes and, perhaps, my unfair opinion of them. I fully realize they were created by God for a specific reason—as all creatures were— including us humans.

Let me now turn back the hands of time—some sixty years—to this side of the ocean, and the fabulous fifties and sixties. Except for the very early fifties when I faced overwhelming challenges in learning the English language, the difficulty in adjusting to a brand new way of life with an enigmatic father, and missing my family back home, life was sweet and exciting, especially when I finished high school, business school, and began earning my own money.

I was still in my early twenties when the roses in my garden—like blooming petunias on a rooftop of previous years—graced my world with their perfumed blossoms. This was my time to experience the joys of youth in American style, delayed by a few years due to unavoidable circumstances, but nonetheless real and exciting.

The anticipation of the well-deserved weekend of fun—after a week-long dedication of giving my best on the job—never failed to make me happy enough to fly in the great blue sky, if wings had been a part of my essence. A new dress for a Saturday dance or a date with a handsome "boy" friend. A church choir rehearsal—Eastern Orthodox—on a Friday night, followed by a pizza get-together on Journal Square in Jersey City. At the end of which we all went our separate ways via the different buses, and we were never afraid—like we would be today—to travel alone and walk several blocks after midnight to our respective homes, happy as larks and looking forward to the following Friday—more singing, pizza, and fun.

Those were the days when young people trusted and respected each other on all levels. When a kiss was just a kiss and never went further. A kiss that began with a gentle peck on the cheek and graduated to a real kiss on the lips, if the friendship continued. The days when young women accepted rides home from young men upon first meeting at a social event or a traditional Saturday night dance—consisting mostly of fast Polkas intermingled with some passionate slow dances—and never felt threatened of being taken advantage of, in payment for favor rendered. That was, if the particular young gentleman was lucky enough to own a car or his parents were kind enough to lend him one for the occasion, if they owned one. When traveling solo to New York City to buy a new dress was not a cause for parents to worry about; I did it on regular basis and lived to tell about it. The thought of potential harm en route to the big city and back home never crossed my mind because the signs were not there. Simply put, the world was moving at a much slower but safer pace.

We earned less money, bought less things, created less clutter, yet appreciated our blessings more than we do today. And we were not desensitized to other's actual plights or ones transmitted by television or radio media because these were few and far between, not what we experience today. Looking back, purchasing a new dress, shoes, or an occasional coat brought joy which lasted until the next major purchase, weeks or even months later. Those were the days when women dressed to the hilt just going to the neighborhood store. And working women wore the Sunday best to their places of employment, including high heels. And when traveling anywhere by bus, train, or plane, or attending houses of worship, women graced their heads with fashionable hats, their bodies with customary suits, dresses or skirts and blouses, their hands with white gloves, and their feet with high heels, but never pants or even casual clothes so prevalent in today's nonchalant world. Pants were unheard of for women in the '40s, '50s, or even '60s. Pants belonged, strictly, to a gentleman's world. And using offensive language in a work place, on television, or radio was reason enough for dismissal. How our world has changed, and not for the better, in my humble opinion.

A small refrigerator and a 13" black and white television—if the family was able to afford them—lasted a mini lifetime. The pride of such extravagant ownership never failed to show up on the family's smiling faces. A manual typewriter was a status symbol in the home to be passed down to the next generation. Its maintenance began and ended with a simple ribbon changing from time to time, and an occasional key-cleaning with rubberized play dough-like substance, fun to roll around in your hands, unlike the computers of today that require constant updating, maintenance, and big money to keep the darn thing current. And we, the users of all these innovations, are supposed to stay calm, cool, and collected—and stress free—because of all the gadgets out there to help us live a better life. I wonder!

Texting is now all the rage. The word is not even in my dictionary. And no, I don't have an e-mail address. I prefer keeping in touch with family and friends via the telephone equipped with every touch-stuff electronic innovation imaginable, or a handwritten, pretty perfumed stationery—not easily found these days, to my regret. I realize life is all about changes and progress must keep on moving forward—and complacency is not an option in our fast-rate, stressed-out society. But did this quick-paced progress and outrageous innovations have to take place in my lifetime? From my senior's view point, the changes I experienced in my seventy-five plus years should have taken at least triple that time. But, at the end of the day, (time) it matters not? Everything in life has a price, and longevity is one of them. Hoorah to the long life at any price. My advice to the young of today is brief and simple:

Work diligently

Love with your heart

Give generously

Be compassionate

Count your blessings

There is an old German saying, "Vee grow too soon oldt, and too late shmart." Don't let this happen to you. Learn as much as you can while you are still young so you can enjoy the long, happy life without regrets for not taking advantage of those golden opportunities presented to you on a "golden" platter in your youth.

# Chapter Four
## What a Difference a Day Makes

Life is all about the right timing of things past, present, and future. The precise time and place when the celestial bodies—the sun, moon, and stars—appear perfectly aligned with each other to the eye of the beholder, especially the young—and the young at heart—who see the world from the perspective of their own spirited youthfulness and boundless energy. That magical time in life that begs to be set free to experience the best life has to offer. True love!

Looking back to my own youth, I must confess there were times when I thought I had found "true love," but time would always prove me wrong—and for a good reason. There was someone special out there meant just for me and "me" for him, but the precise moment for that enlightenment, and the eventual lifetime commitment, was not ready to be revealed until the two of us were ready to commit to each other.

One and foremost moment still clear and dear to my heart fifty-some years later, is the moment and place I saw my longtime friend, John, no longer as "just" a friend but someone beyond ordinary friend-ship. It had happened when I least expected such a profound change of feelings. Having experienced this amazing transformation under most unlikely circumstances, I feel justified to stand by the quote: "There are no coincidences in life." Life is all about the right timing rather than coincidences in my humble opinion.

My Prince Charming—unlike the hero of the fairytale *Cinderella* by Charles Perrault—did not come riding on a white horse, wearing his heart on his sleeve, or arrogantly circling my house to draw attention to himself in his new car, the Ford Falcon, he had recently purchased. I was on the way home from my usual Saturday shopping spree on Newark Avenue in Jersey City—a mecca for shoppers in my day (and perhaps still today) and only blocks of walking distance from our respective homes, my friend John's and mine—when the unthinkable took place.

This long-ago April day in 1960 was delightfully sunny and warm, perfect for walking and enjoying the pleasing spring cool breezes bestowed upon the downtown Jersey City residents by the two nearby well-known rivers, the New York's East River and the Hudson River on the Jersey side. I spotted John in the parking space he was privileged to use, owned by the church we both attended, and where I sang in the choir for the last thirteen years—the Eastern Orthodox Church, dating back to the beginning of the twentieth century and a historical site to be cherished and preserved—which today is, for time immemorial. I sighted John deeply absorbed in admiring his pride and joy shiny black car, decided to say a quick hello, and be on my way with my treasure, anxious to get home and model the new dress for my parents to get their approval, and praise, for spending my hard-earned money wisely. John's and mine occasional meetings in the past were always limited to a brief "How are you?" and "See you around," so I expected the same this time.

"It's nice to see you, Luba. You look very nice as always, but especially today in that white spring coat, high heels, matching pocketbook, and white gloves to boot." I always dressed up in my best when leaving the house for work, for church, or even to go shopping (everybody did in those days), but John, evidently, never noticed me before this day. These first-time unexpected compliments, spoken by the quiet, reserved John—the art teacher—left me speechless for a brief moment. But I quickly collected my thoughts and returned the courtesy.

"Thank you, John. You look very nice too, and so does your new car!" John smiled and asked if I wanted to take a ride in his car, some time. Before I could reply, "I'll keep your offer in mind," John confidently uttered the words that shocked me.

"Better yet, would you—could you—go on a date with me. I mean, a dinner and a dance at a place I'll keep to myself for now, just so that I can surprise you, that is, if you accept my invitation for a date."

"I am surprised already, and can hardly wait for the rest of it," I heard myself say, not fully realizing I had literally jumped at the chance for a date with my casual friend, John. Talking about the right timing, I was not romantically attached to anyone.

Our first date was to Swiss Chalet, an entertainment establishment known—but not to me prior to that first date—for its great food and "Oompah-pah" music, John revealed to me during the dinner, which consisted of a palette of flavors indigenous to the German culture, and dancing to the "Oompah-pah" live band till the wee hours of the morning. And we so enjoyed that rhythmic, fast repetition of steps similar to the Polka tempo we both knew well, I secretly wished the evening could have gone on forever, because we were having so much fun. But like everything in life, nothing lasts forever. This evening was nearing the end, and I didn't know if another date with John would be in the picture.

With a peck on the cheek, John said good night, asked me for another date, and when I said "I'd love to go out with you again," he handed me a small package and, with a wide smile on his handsome face, motioned for me to open it. Being careful not to appear too anxious to see the contents inside, I slowly and gently removed the colorful wrapping paper. My eyes widened and a tear or two unavoidably rolled down my cheeks when the unexpected, most thoughtful gift, revealed itself. The lovely miniature, handcrafted replica of the Swiss Chalet we had just left, and where the "true love"—unbeknownst to us at the time—must have taken root, while we were immensely enjoying ourselves. And this heart-melting, fuzzy feeling lingered on through the night and became even stronger when we were saying good night—or rather, good morning.

As soon as I had awaken few hours later, I reached for the pen resting on the desk next to the bed in my room, and on the bottom of the miniature Swiss Chalet replica lovingly scripted the date I received it, from whom, and on what occasion, and vowed to save it for posterity. I knew right then the previous night's momentous date was merely the first of many to come. Our time together had come, because that was what God wanted for us—in sickness and in health, for better and for worse. The wise words spoken by the well-known actor of my day, Yul Brynner, in "The King and I" movie, "What shall be will be," echoed through my mind and I was completely accepting—and ready—for the challenges those words might have prophesized.

John and I dated throughout the spring, summer, and fall of 1960, and all four seasons of 1961. We took tennis lessons together in Jersey City's well-known Lincoln Park, went bowling on Saturday nights after dinners out. And, yes, we argued from time to time. Some of our disagreements were the results of our differences and appeared serious enough to give them our all. Differences bound to surface when two people in love begin to think about their future together. Two people bearing different DNAs, raised by dissimilar sets of parents, in different parts of the world in this case. Some trivial arguments that would quickly dissipate or settle to our individual satisfactions, and brought us even closer in minds and hearts.

For Christmas 1961, John presented me with a one-of-a-kind, hand-crafted Christmas tree (made by him and his students in school), small enough for a tabletop decoration, large enough to fill my heart with plenty of love for John to think of our relationship as special and serious. John succeeded in stealing my heart, and I succumbed to his tenderness to think of no one else but him. Our longtime, casual friendship stealthily turned to indestructible love. Love, strong enough to face our challenges ahead courageously, and turn the mistakes we made in the process into valuable lessons that taught us how not to repeat them. Yes, we made mistakes—we all do—but if we learn from them, that's education, free of charge. Live, keep on learning, and don't fear mistakes. That's my humble advice to the young people of today.

Our engagement on St. Valentine's Day in 1962 was the highlight of my life. We were alone in a fabulous restaurant chosen by my soon-to-be fiancé, John. My forever friend and husband-to-be, reached deep into his pocket and pulled out a small, blue velvet box which he smilingly handed over to me. Very slowly, I proceeded to open the box, being careful not to show too much emotion in case the little blue box didn't contain what I thought it might—an engagement ring. I didn't want to appear too presumptuous. The thoughts of possible disappointment were quickly put to rest as the beautiful engagement ring came to view. Tears of joy began to roll down my cheeks when the love of my life removed the ring from the box, squeezed my trembling hands, gently placed the white gold, solitaire diamond ring on my finger and asked me to marry him. I threw my arms around my fiancé and—without hesitation—said "Yes, I would be honored to be your wife." My thoughtful husband-to-be thought of everything to make that special evening even more wonderful and memorable, if that was ever possible.

As soon as he slipped the ring on my finger, an announcement of our engagement rang out from the overhead speaker, and we were asked to step on the dance floor (just the two of us while others watched). We danced to our favorite song by the immortal Elvis Presley, "I Can't Help Falling in Love with You," requested in advance by now my fiancé. This epic classic became our favorite song through the years, to which we loved to dance, especially on the anniversaries of our engagement.

The rest of that stupendous evening we spent dancing and holding each other close. From time to time, we both playfully checked to see if the ring was really on my finger to make sure this moment was actually happening and not just a dream we secretly wished would come true. Our parents gave us their undivided blessings and enough love to last a lifetime. My soon-to-be husband, John, knew my love for the mountains, open spaces, and nature in general, so—in addition to the beautiful engagement ring—he presented me with an original country-scene painting, crafted by the master painter himself, my fiancé and future husband, John.

I, too, showered him with presents to mark this special day when we became engaged. There were gold cuff links, initiated gold tie bar, and a jacket I knew he admired in the store window. But I would be remiss if I left out the wedding gift from my sweetheart for our upcoming wedding—a string of lustrous cultured pearls and matching earrings I proudly wore on our wedding, treasure to this day, and wear only on special occasions.

In retrospect, our celebration of love—our engagement—was the special moment in time that for us, blessedly, would come but once, and surpassed even our elaborate wedding festivities, since on our wedding day, we felt compelled to share ourselves with some three hundred invited guests, and see to every detail that everyone was properly treated and entertained because they were there to honor us. Unlike our engagement when we felt there was only "us" in this great big world of ours.

Looking back, we are grateful today for the large wedding celebration we were privileged to have (courtesy of my generous parents), despite all the work and some confusion that might have sneaked in—we had to deal with—when we were not looking.

Our wedding pictures with loved ones by our side, remain a constant reminder of that special day in our lives, and indirectly theirs also. Loved ones! Many of whom are no longer with us but remain frozen in time and in our hearts forever. We were married on a partially cloudy Saturday at four o'clock in the afternoon on October 6, 1962 at St. Peter & Paul Orthodox Church on Grand Street, in Jersey City, New Jersey, where we both worshipped and ultimately became friends. We were married with all the regalia and finery distinctive to the wedding ceremonies in an Eastern Orthodox Church rich in traditions. Our first dance as husband and wife was to the tune of "You Are My Sunshine."

As I write this chapter of the sequel to my memoir, *Blossoms on a Rooftop,* I am reminded of the song I loved listening to in my much younger days, "Where Have All the Flowers Gone" by Peter, Paul, and Mary, the well-known trio of yesteryears. How grateful I am that "flowers" were never "gone"out of our married life, and we never grew too old to appreciate and draw strength from them as we continued on our "together" journey through life as each others' sunshine.

# Chapter Five
# Our Own Place

The third-floor, three-room apartment—in a complex of thirty-some families, brown stone dwelling in Elizabeth, New Jersey, about twenty miles away from our parents' homes in Jersey City, New Jersey, with whom we lived until we married—was the place where we would begin our new life together as husband and wife. With wedding reception over, we gratefully bid our guests a fond farewell, embraced our jubilant parents, and kissed their hands in thanksgiving for their enduring love and unwavering nurturing through the years. Our parents—my mother and father and my new husband's widowed mother, my new mother-in-law—in return, jointly sprinkled holy water over us, placed their hands on our heads, and offered prayers to God that He protect and guide us throughout this lifetime journey called marriage. Upon the completion of the ceremonial formalities, sumptuous dinner, an evening of dancing, and traditional wedding blessings, the time had arrived for us to gratefully bid our guests a fond farewell, and head for "our own place." How exciting!

What distinguished "our first place" from other rentals in the vicinity—close enough to our jobs and appeared more rural than any other available place—was a piece of public property across the street from the apartment. It was only a small, grassy triangle enhanced by ornamental late summer bloomers around a fledging tree, and two park benches where we imagined ourselves relaxing after work, that convinced us this was the apartment for us, because it brought us closer to country living we both yearned for. The varieties of seasonal flower beds hugging the three sides of the building and a small courtyard in the back, overlooking the neighbor's grassy lot, helped seal the deal.

We climbed the three flights of marbleized stairs hanging on, for dear life, to a bagful of wedding envelopes containing monetary gifts along with best wishes for a blessed life together. My new husband opened the door to our unpretentious "love nest," picked me up and carried me over the threshold, as was customarily done by the newly-weds of our time, and perhaps still today. Inside, the apartment was tastefully furnished and decorated according to each of our fervors. A narrow hallway led to an eat-in kitchen with a single window enhanced by a crisscross, white nylon curtain matching other window-treatments throughout the apartment. Opposite the kitchen, to the left, was a spacious living-dining room combination with double windows. To the right of the kitchen was a full-size bathroom, opposite of which was the one and only bedroom with another double window. A clothes closet in the hallway completed the apartment—small in size but large enough for a starting couple with enough love in their hearts to make it a real home for the time being.

While we packed the suitcases for the much anticipated, barely a full week honeymoon trip to Virginia, we rehashed the events of our wedding: some breathtaking moments, others mixed with unfath-omable emotions, and still others with confusion. First and foremost, I needed to apologize to my new husband for keeping him waiting at the altar close to an hour which made him think that things between us—for no known reason to him—had gone awry and there would be no wedding, after all the preparations and high anticipations. What possible explanation could he give to the invited guests who traveled distances to celebrate this special time with us when he didn't know the answer to the dilemma himself?

It was simply a defective zipper on one of the bridesmaids' gowns that delayed the ceremony. A zipper that needed to be replaced by a seamstress in another town where the gowns were custom-made, which caused the delay and confusion. But, as the saying goes, "all's well that ends well." But I couldn't help question, why the Murphy's law—"If something is going to go wrong, will go wrong"—had to happen on my watch and my moment of happiness?

I arrived in church with the entire entourage late, but ready for the greatest commitment of my life, and was given away by my older brother, Michael, who took our disabled dear father's place. Michael also danced the father-daughter dance with me, while my father stood by and watched.

With misty eyes, we recalled the special moments of this never-to-be-forgotten day. For our first drink as husband and wife, we sipped red wine from a common cup. Our first steps as husband and wife, was a three-round ceremonial walk around the table of oblation facing the altar, with officiating priest holding our right hands bound by a white handkerchief and the maid of honor and best man holding crowns over our heads, symbolizing king and queen of our own little kingdom from this day forward. We still have the tied handkerchief—slipped from our right hands with its knot in place—tucked away with our other treasured mementos to remind us of the day we became one.

The traditional wedding ceremony, according to the Eastern Orthodox rite is long but unbelievably beautiful and meaningful, especially when accompanied by an a cappella choir, which most are. When it is over, you know you are married for better or for worse.

In the church vestibule, our beloved parents were waiting to greet us and give us their blessings for a long and happy life together. We, in turn, embraced them individually and thanked them for their sacrifices on our behalf, before receiving the many invited guests waiting in line. Outside, the low, dark clouds over our heads threatened imminent downpour, but nothing could dissuade the well-wishers in front of the church to toss handfuls of rice in our direction as we smilingly stood atop the church steps and the photographers snapped pictures of us and our wedding party for posterity. This indelible long-gone day—October 6, 1962—distinguishes itself from all others in our married life, because for us, it could happen but once and we knew it from the start.

We packed my husband's Ford Falcon car (now ours) and were on our way to celebrate our marriage. Everything seemed so perfect and so right, except for one particular moment in church when we were taking our vows. I heard someone crying out loud and realized it was my dear heart mother. What was the reason for this outburst of emotions? This was completely out of character for my mother's calm and collected demeanor. Did something happen to my ailing father, John's mom, a family member, or a guest? I desperately wanted to turn around and see for myself what was happening, but knew this would be the wrong thing to do. This was our moment to hold and to cherish for as long as we both shall live. And nothing should take its precedence.

Less than a year into our marriage, my dear mother could no longer keep her terminal illness to herself—an invasion of her body by an incurable cancer that eventually took her life at age sixty-one. As painful as it must have been for her to suffer alone while we were planning my wedding, she decided to keep the secret to herself and share it only with my father for as long as was possible, so I could begin my life with my husband in peace and tranquility. Unfortunately, my mother's well-intentioned protection on my behalf was not worth the shock that rattled my world when the inevitable confronted me, and I was not as prepared as I should have been to deal with the reality of it, had I known about it right along.

"Virginia is for lovers!" I had seen beach towels imprinted with such logos and also billboards, but paid little attention to the claims, thinking such claims were simply for advertising purposes to lure the potential visitors to Virginia. I was wrong! I was also mistaken when I thought the lyrics and the spectacular natural scenery from the classic motion picture, "The Sound of Music"—primarily the excerpt, "The hills are alive with the sound of music"—were merely a fantasy; the film producer's figment of imagination exclusively for entertainment, with no real facts to back them up. Our wedding trip to Virginia proved me wrong on both counts.

Living in the city for well over a decade, working long hours in a busy office, and attending evening classes at a prestigious school— The Seton Hall University—I became accustomed to this lifestyle and accepted it as if there was no other. Such as, the rolling hills, the meadows strewn with wild flowers and grazing cattle, silvery streams leisurely babbling to no particular destinations, majestic trees in the green fields—and by the roads—waving their umbrella-like branches as if to say: "Welcome to the country travelers! See and feel what we see and feel!" The sky of the bluest hue, the sun's warmest rays, and only enough rain to appreciate the difference.

My fascination with all the beauty around us prompted my husband, John, to make frequent stops along the way to take pictures, especially of the trees. The ones that, for me, transcended the time and space and brought me back to my long-gone childhood in the Carpathian Mountains—the Lemko region in southeastern Poland—and its grandeur. For me, personally, this was a trip made in heaven with power enough to even stop admiring the white gold wedding band on my finger to match my engagement ring from time to time, as well as an additional gold wedding band for each of us for everyday wear—mine inscribed "John to Luba" and John's "Luba to John," which continue to remind us of our wedding day to this day, because we are never without them. The picturesque country scenes and the majestic trees were only the beginning of what was still awaiting us on this unforgettable honeymoon trip.

The grandeur and the splendor of the Shenandoah National Park/Skyline Drive through the Blue Ridge Mountains defied then—and still today—the words in my vocabulary to justly describe the transcendence of mind and soul when "mine" eyes first beheld its magnificence. The lyrics borrowed from the first stanza of "America the Beautiful" anthem by Katharine Lee Bates in 1913, vividly and movably identify with my deep emotions at that moment in time:

> O beautiful for spacious skies,
> For amber waves of grain,
> For purple mountain majesties
> Above the fruited plain!
> America! America! God shed His grace on thee,
> And crown thy good with brotherhood
> From sea to shining sea!

Next on our itinerary of places to see were the Luray Caverns. Wonders below the ground! Not even in my wildest dreams could I have imagined such miracles of nature and the genius of human mind: Well-paved walkways stretching throughout the cavernous rooms, some as high as ten stories; enormous columns and crystal clear pools; the world's largest musical instrument, the Great Stalactite Organ—

created from a deposit of calcium carbonate, resembling icicles on sides of the cave. A must see if your travels take you to Virginia.

Last but certainly not least, was another national wonder—The Natural Bridge, which Thomas Jefferson called the "most sublime of nature's works." We were there to witness the presentation of the "Drama of Creation" with lighting effects and music beneath the bridge, given daily at dusk. And some still say there is no God?

One week in celebration of our wedding didn't seem enough, but that was all the vacation we had. It was time to journey back home and to face reality of our new life in our own Garden State of New Jersey, where our loved ones and jobs were waiting for us. We were excited to see the "WELCOME TO NEW JERSEY" sign, and anxiously awaited the one for Elizabeth where "our first place" as husband and wife happened to be. It finally appeared! But where was the street our apartment was located at? We only knew the way to our apartment from our respective homes in Jersey City and not from the highways and byways we traveled upon to and from Virginia. We needed directions to get home and stopped at the first gas station off a myriad of side streets to purchase a map for the City of Elizabeth, parked the car on the side of the road, and searched for our street. On the way we encountered a few unanticipated detours but pressed on. We finally found our way home and were greeted by the shining light in the kitchen we inadvertently left on in anxious anticipation of our trip.

The honeymoon trip itself had ended, but our life together had just begun. It was back to work and reality in the morning. Reality different from the one we were used to, but very exciting and challenging. "Our own place" was a three-room humble apartment, but to our hearts and souls, it was a castle fit for a king and queen. Us! King and queen of our own little kingdom.

# Chapter Six
# "We've Only Just Begun"

---------------------------------------

*"Sharing horizons that are new to us,*
*Watching the signs along the way,*
*Talking it over just the two of us,*
*Working together day to day*
*Together."*
(Third stanza from lyrical composition,
"We've Only Just Begun)

---------------------------------------

The foregoing classic, melodically and lyrically intoxicating arrangement, was immortalized in a song, "We've Only Just Begun," by Paul Williams and Roger Nichols, sung by the well-known brother-sister duo of my time, The Carpenters, and still celebrated today. It clearly personifies our own aspirations for the life we've started together. Together—as in "us," "we," and "ours." Could there be a more pleasing sound when two people in love decide to share their lives together and work for the same goals? Through two simple words but well thought through—"I do"—we evolved to a lifetime team, ready to tackle any stumbling blocks along the way and turn them into stepping stones for building a marriage foundation strong enough to withstand other obstacles bound to cross our paths as we traveled on through the unfolding years of our lives into the future—*together.*

Sooner than we expected, the reality of life caught up with us and nudged us to let go of the honeymoon moments in the sun, tuck away their treasured memories—for the time being—and face the responsibilities and challenges that come with having a "place of our own."

Early Saturday morning of our second week wedding anniversary, I tiptoed out of bed so I wouldn't disturb my sleeping husband and quietly left the apartment for the beauty parlor appointment to have my hair done in anticipation of a dinner/dance that evening—hopefully—in a fancy restaurant my husband would have chosen to surprise me. The surprise was not what I expected. On my return home with my hair sculptured in latest style, my nails painted bright pink to match my lipstick, I found my husband fumbling through the dresser drawer for a clean pair of socks and underwear. Reality hit me like a ton of bricks.

Practically, everything we owned in terms of daily essentials was in our "dirty" clothes bin. In a feeble attempt to show my new husband, that things were not as bad as they seemed, I ran to the kitchen and opened the refrigerator door, hoping to find enough stuff in there to fix a nice brunch for the two of us. The only things—I still remember—staring back at me were an unopened bottle of ketchup and some mustard. All other edibles we had purchased in the familiar Jersey City food store and brought to our apartment in Elizabeth were used up. Our cupboards were bare in every way. We had not food-shopped, cleaned the apartment, or had done any wash since we moved in after the wedding—prior to our honeymoon—two weeks earlier. Every evening—after work—we prepared dinner (while the supplies lasted), cleaned up afterwards, reminisced about the wedding and the honeymoon, and overlooked everything else that needed attention, and there was no one to pick up where we left off—like our parents back in our respective homes in Jersey City. We were now on our own and responsible for ourselves.

We decided to, first, grab a quick lunch in some neighborhood luncheonette before tackling the necessary domestic projects, one by one. With full tummies and happy spirits, the teamwork had begun!

We sat at the kitchen table enhanced by a vase of artificial, white chrysanthemums, reminiscent of fresh flowers that made up my wedding bouquet. A mutually agreed upon list of things to do after work and on weekends soon appeared, posted on the refrigerator door. I volunteered to prepare evening meals and John offered to do the supper dishes. So far so good!

The dreary-in-appearance laundromat we carried our bin of "dirty" laundry to (there was no washer and dryer in our apartment or building) later on that afternoon, was not where we both wished to celebrate our two-week young wedding anniversary, but we did what was necessary and still enjoyed the moment, because we were together. Once the place emptied out, and our machines and dryers were the only ones turning and twisting the clothing inside, we whispered to each other, "Let's dance." And we danced to the legendary Elvis Presley's classic, "I Can't Stop Loving You"; the lyrics and melody we both knew and loved. It was late afternoon by the time the last dryer came to a stop, but our day was still not done.

With sweet-smelling clothes neatly folded and placed in their appropriate storage places in the apartment, next on the "to-do" list was the task of food-shopping for the week; because the refrigerator remained empty and no "fairy godmother" was about to come to our rescue, we unanimously agreed. Outside, the autumn sun was nearing the horizon and the cloudy skies around appeared ready to let go of rain, and maybe lots of it, but that didn't dissuade us from accomplishing our next task—shopping for food and choosing what we both liked. Safely home, we unpacked the shopping bags and set the table for two for a simple but satisfying supper—purchased ready-made—embellished by a bottle of dinner wine leftover from the wedding reception, to toast our two-week wedding anniversary. Before we settled in for the night, we dusted the furniture and vacuumed the floors. There was still enough wine left in the bottle for one more toast, this time, to "teamwork."

The next morning—Sunday—we showered, dressed, and rushed out of the apartment to be on time for church in Jersey City, where we were married two weeks earlier. After church, we visited our respective families and—on this particular Sunday—shared with them the memories of our wedding trip and presented them with "thank you" gifts for their sacrifices—and unconditional love—through the years. We continued attending our homebase church in Jersey City and visiting our parents (and families) afterwards until life took us, and them, in different directions years later.

Not everything in "our first place" met our expectations. The grassy triangle across the street from our apartment with two park benches, a fledgling tree encircled by blooming flowers, where we envisioned ourselves relaxing after work and on weekends, proved to be an empty promise. From our one and only experience, instead of relaxing and watching the world go by as we imagined, we watched bumper-to-bumper merging traffic. As October turned to November with December on its heels, the roses and other blooming plants around the perimeter of the apartment building withered, and soon became obliterated by a blanket of snowflakes that unexpectedly fell down from the sky one dark night. The apartment, inside, was getting colder and colder with each passing winter day. The heat would stop channeling in through the pipes at a certain time of the night—or late evening—regardless of the temperature outside. How grateful we were for the featherbed we received as a wedding present from our parents, and the warm sweaters in our wardrobes we wore to work and—on frigidly cold nights—to bed.

One comforting thought remained constant in our minds: If winter is here, can spring be far away? Spring! The word alone made our hearts sing, especially since we lived almost within a walking (long walk) distance from the Warinanco Park in Elizabeth, where azalea, rhododendrons, and cherry blossoms—around the lake—dazzled visitors with their kaleidoscopic colors every spring. We were fortunate to have witnessed the nature at its best at Warinanco Park the Easter before our October wedding of the same year. So, when we shivered in our apartment during that first winter and envisioned a scorching summer days and nights ahead—because there would be no air conditioning or a window unit—in our outmoded apartment due to insufficient electrical power, we remembered the park, and our worries about long, hot summer ahead would subside.

# Chapter Seven
## Some Things Are Meant to Be

Be it ever so humble, there is no place like home for the holidays, even if the home happens to be a rented apartment. With Thanksgiving holiday a distant memory—and gloomy, short, winter days overshadowing the happy memories of our wedding and honeymoon—the thoughts of approaching Christmas and joyful celebrations with family and friends in our own place, sprinkled our three-month-young marriage with new excitement and anticipation. Our winter-weary, subdued moods seemed instantaneously revitalized at the sound of the initial piped-in, cheery holiday music in the shopping center near us, and our eyes beheld the first seasonal displays of colorful lights in store windows and on the neighboring evergreen trees and lawns. The aroused to action shoppers—with wide-eyed children in tow—helped solidify the reality of our first Christmas as husband and wife. The rite of passage to begin forming holiday traditions of our own—building upon the ones our parents passed on to us—which would best work for us and our future family we hoped to have one day, had started.

A tabletop, fledgling live spruce was what we finally decided on for our first Christmas tree. But not before I expressed my wish for a forest-scent Christmas tree that was a tradition in my homeland of

Lemkovyna in the Carpathian Mountains where I grew up. And John let his reasons known for an artificial Christmas tree that would shed no needles and remind him of Christmases at home with his family. In the end, we were both happy in having that little bit of nature from the outside brought in to the inside, from which a heavenly aroma wafted throughout all the three rooms of our apartment until we took the tree down after January 7th, Christmas day according to the Julian calendar we observed then, and some Eastern Orthodox Christian Churches still do today, including the one we attend in Elizabeth, New Jersey.

The decorations on our tree consisted of a few colorful glass ornaments, a string of electric lights, and enough silver tinsel to create a glittering and sparkling sight from all angles of the living room, where we planned on entertaining guests during the holiday season. The tree was set on a red velvet skirt upon which the traditional nativity figures rested that continue—to this day—to grace our home at Christmastime in defiance of age, time, and place—like the people who celebrated that first Christmas with us, close to five decades ago. We wish they were still with us along with our precious nativity set. But we are grateful for the time we had with them, and the timeless memories and heartprints they left behind for us to treasure.

The holiday season seemed the perfect time to make a few friends in the apartment by having an open house with finger foods and drinks one day. We posted a general invitation on our mail box—where all the other mailboxes were located—and distributed individual invitations to each apartment. Incidentally, the mailboxes in those days could never accommodate the large volumes of mail we receive today, including slews of magazines and "junk" mail that needs to be discarded. Inside of "yesteryear" mailboxes, one would find mainly an occasional personal letter from distant relatives or friends which never failed to make your day more interesting and—now and then—a piece of correspondence that needed attention. How the times have changed!

We patiently waited for people to show up at our planned get-together and introduce ourselves to them and themselves to us, since we hadn't met anyone in the three-month period we had lived there, except for the landlady who kept strictly to apartment business. The specified time for this open house event was nearing the end and so was our patience. We were convinced this attempt to get to know some people in the apartment and—hopefully—make a few friends at the same time was a futile effort from the get-go, and began putting things away with utmost disappointment. Lo and behold, there came a faint knock on the door which brought us to our feet. We both ran to see who was on the other side of the door. Our eyes became fixed—in surprise—on an elderly lady with an armful of brochures and what looked like a slew of small packages and bottles, samples of something she was selling, we presumed, things we probably wouldn't be interested in, anyway. Such waste of our time and hers!

"Avon calling!" the lady announced with a smile. A smile that would soon disappear from her face—we thought—since we had no intentions of buying anything that day, especially things she was selling. We were awaiting guests and not salespeople, unaware of the fact she lived in the apartment building and probably knew most of the residents there. We invited her in against our better judgment and reluctantly showed her to the serving table. She smilingly freed her hands and arms of the items that were weighing her down, and helped herself to whatever was still not put away. The evening concluded with three happy people. The Avon lady, because she sold more stuff to us than she—probably—ever had to anyone at one single visit; and the two of us, because, we finally met someone in the apartment that would be calling on us again and again and, hopefully, share the news she collected from other tenants about the apartment business we would, otherwise, not be privileged to know. We now had one friend in the apartment that continued to call on us frequently, and always with a wide smile and juicy news that made us smile too. During the remainder of this first Christmas season in our first place, we were graced with visits from our families and friends who came at different times—invited and uninvited—but were all welcomed with pleasure, joy, and, pride just the same.

We survived the first winter in our cold apartment, and now that warm weather—and eventually hot—was fast approaching, we questioned if we would be any better off? Meanwhile, enjoy spring and all growing and blooming things, including the one in my stomach. We were in the family way! But the early signs heralding the blessed event were not apparent. Concerned about the intermittent bleeding, I decided to call on our longtime family doctor in Jersey City to help me with the problem, even though I knew full well gynecology was not within his realm of expertise. But I couldn't imagine myself being intimately examined by a doctor I just met. I realized—almost too late—some things require the handling of an expert and should be left to the experts. My folly almost cost us a precious life, looming within my body, we were praying for.

Trust and respect are the key factors in any relationship. I am grateful, today, that we had them in our marriage and that I put them to the test at the most crucial time of our lives and the life of a tiny, struggling being wanting to be born, against all odds.

"You are not going to the hospital in the morning for a surgery we know nothing about. We need time to think about this and get a second opinion, and perhaps a third one too, before I will agree to it," my husband sputtered as he hit the table with his fist which almost brought me to tears, because that was so uncharacteristic of his behavior.

"Why don't you understand how crucial this surgery is for us to have children in the future? I tearfully questioned. "Anyway, the operation is already scheduled for seven o'clock in the morning, so how can I pull out?"

I desperately pleaded to make him understand my dilemma. "It's only an overnight stay, and I'll be back the next day. You don't even have to be there." I reasoned with him.

But his argument remained the same. "You are not going! You are not going!" He kept on repeating as he checked his pocket telephone book and began dialing numbers. Not long after, his demeanor changed. My husband—as I was privileged to know him—was back.

"Get ready, I found someone to see us! One of the teachers in my school has a friend-doctor who agreed to see us right now. Hurry! Hurry! Before he closes the office for the day."

The doctor's office was not far from our apartment, so it took us only minutes to get there, but for us, this God-sent visit to this angel-in-disguise doctor proved priceless. He simply looked into my eyes and smilingly declared. "You are pregnant! Let me call my good friend, Dr. Whitken, and ask him if he could squeeze you in to physically confirm my visual diagnosis. Dr. Whitken's office is nearby and my nurse will give you directions," he said and continued. "I don't want to examine you because that will be Dr. Whitken's job, as well as the follow-up visits from this point on, until the birth of your baby and thereafter."

A baby! We're having a baby! We both exclaimed as we embraced each other—and the doctor too, because he was our savior—with tears of joy trickling down our cheeks.

The examination by Dr. Whitken—a favor to Dr. Spivack—assisted by his nurse, took only minutes, and the fear of being intimately examined by a doctor I had not seen before didn't even enter my mind. After all, he was a doctor and well-prepared for the job he was doing.It finally dawned on me.

We both listened to the baby's strong heartbeat and could hardly believe this was really happening, and even questioned the reality of it all. What a difference those few rewarding hours made in our lives! Some things are meant to be and so was our baby, yet, to-be.

"You are about two months into the pregnancy," Dr. Whitken smilingly announced and continued. "I'll be monitoring the baby's progress on monthly basis, so make your next appointment with the receptionist for one month from today. Don't hesitate to call if questions should arise and the satisfactory answers are not found in the brochures you'll be taking home with you. Meanwhile, take life easier, take naps when you can, or, at least, put your feet up whenever possible." Dr. Whitken advised.

We could hardly wait to tell everyone and anyone willing to listen to our amazing but true story—especially our dear parents—about the baby on the way that almost wasn't. To this day, the reality of how close we came to losing our firstborn precious baby still brings me to tears. But we both take comfort in knowing that Somebody up there was watching out for us as well as the cherished new life growing inside of me who was meant to be born, grow, and bloom along with other flowers of the world. Our children! Our gifts from above! Let us cherish them forever!

For us, June roses of that memorable year of 1963 were blooming everywhere, even if there were none to be seen prior to this astounding news that a precious baby of ours was on the way. This was a story with a happy ending—thanks be to God!

# Chapter Eight
## Paradox of Life

The expression "into each life some rain must fall" is one universal truth no one escapes on their journey through life. Sooner or later, we all must face rainy days in one shape or another, personally, nationally, or even worldwide. Take, for instance, the devastating earthquakes, tsunamis, tornadoes—and who could ever forget the worst terror-attack on America on 9/11/2001—our nation and the world suffered in the young twenty-first century alone. It's mind-boggling and beyond human understanding! Mother Nature isn't always fair, nor are the humans (if you could call them that) who will take their own lives to kill others for no other reason than different orientations. How sad that humans are capable of stooping so low!

One such stormy day that distinguishes itself from all others in my memory, is the gunning down of our beloved president—John Fitzgerald Kennedy—that stunned the nation and the world, and changed the American history going forward. Forever!

I was on a maternity leave of absence from my job at the time of this national tragedy and spent my days in quiet solitude preparing for the baby. I busied myself with necessary household chores and—for pleasure—I picked up a passion for knitting and crocheting adorable baby things in happy anticipation of the little one soon to make us a family of three. Growing up in the Carpathian Mountains—out of necessity—I learned to knit and crochet at a young age. I made sweaters, shawls, hats, scarves and such, out of homegrown and spun flax plants. We planted flax seeds in spring and harvested the mature plants in the fall. We then turned the dry flax stalks—by special processing—to yarn, suitable for knitting and crocheting. Our ingenuity kept us warm during the long winter months and made us self-sufficient in terms of clothing.

How blessed I felt now, sitting on a comfortable couch surrounded by baby magazines featuring easy-to-follow knitting and crocheting patterns/directions and colorful skeins of soft to the touch, delicate baby yarn, ready to be turned to cute baby things—sweater sets, hats, booties, and crib-size afghans. The mere thought of a peacefully sleeping little one, dressed and wrapped in the baby things I created out of love brought chills of joy down my spine, as I imagined (and desperately wanted) this gift from above in my arms way before the baby's due date. The saying, "be careful what you wish for" turned to reality I would soon question, but never regretted.

On November 21, 1963, everything was still right with our nation and the world. And no one—beside the perpetrator—knew what dreadful tragedy was about to befall us. And no one—beside the killer—saw the dark clouds gathering over Dallas, Texas, soon to let go of the torrential rains that would engulf our country. And it all happened in a blink of an eye!

The next day, **November 22, 1963,** I was ironing my husband's white cotton shirts (collars and cuffs heavily starched to give them texture)—a fresh shirt for each new day of school to wear under his jacket—which was mandated by the school's dress code for male teachers at the time. My thoughts were preoccupied with smoothing out every stubborn crease and wrinkle from the pile of lightly sprinkled—for easier ironing—bunch of shirts on the chair in front of me, awaiting their turns. I often wondered—as I did then—how my elderly mother-in-law, Anastasia, with her hands knurled from arthritis and still working full time in New York City cleaning offices, handled this tedious job for her son and never complained? I didn't complain either, but this was, certainly, not what I enjoyed doing. What made this weekly task more tolerable for me was listening to the tranquil music played on the radio and visualizing myself caressing the baby and watching it grow through different stages. Will it be a boy or a girl? Not that it really mattered. But still I wondered. I even imagined myself with twins, and what a blessing that would be! In those days, there was no technology to tell the sex of the baby or if there was one or two.

Soon, my concentration on the wrinkled shirts and the baby came to an abrupt stop. Coming from the hallway adjacent to our apartment door where I was ironing was clearly audible sobbing, which appeared to be coming from a distraught male. This strange noise filled me with fear and curiosity. I placed the iron on a heat-resistant appliance and— just to be safe—disconnected the iron. I opened the door as far as the safety latch would allow me, peaked out through the opening and listened. What I saw and heard stunned me and chased away any fears and hesitations I might have had about opening the door all the way. I had to take a chance. Something strange was happening that had never happened before. My eyes widened and my heart began to race. Standing next to a dripping mop and a bucket of water, was a devastated African-American cleaning man who seemingly needed help. And quick! I could call the police, a thought came to my mind. But before I ran back to the apartment to make that call, I heard the man speak. The words I heard from this individual's quivering lips—his face stained with tears—brought me to an emotional shock. Words that will forever remain frozen in my mind!

**"They killed him! President Kennedy is dead! Oh, God of mercy, help us!"**

I didn't question where he heard this because, deep down, I knew it was true. No one could make up a story of such magnitude and severity. I felt a fainting spell coming on—a frightening moment I remembered well when it happened to me in church earlier in my pregnancy. This can't be happening again. Not now! I must be strong for this grief-stricken individual, for myself and, of course, for our precious baby who begged for consideration by kicking inside my tummy more vigorously than it ever had before. I grabbed this gentle man's hand and he grabbed mine, so we could support each other in an effort to somehow process this horrendous news and not let it tear at our hearts more than it already had. We had to get control of our emotional shock.

Soon, my husband, John—breathless from running three flights of stairs—joined us. He was dismissed from school, along with all teachers and students, as soon as this tragic news was announced over the intercom. The three of us held on to each other as we wept. We didn't know this dear individual's name we were holding onto for dear life, nor did he know us, but we became one in heart and soul because of our common loss and grief.

"President John Fitzgerald Kennedy was killed by an assassin's bullets as his motorcade wound through Dallas, Texas. He was the youngest man elected president, he was the youngest to die." His untimely death at age forty-six, left behind a grieving nation and the world; a loving wife, Jacqueline Bouvier Kennedy; and two young children, Caroline and John. Who, from my generation, doesn't remember the three-year-old John, saluting his father as the motorcade—carrying the president's coffin—passed by him, his black-veiled mother, "Jackie," older sister, Caroline, and multitude of grief-stricken people standing nearby, weeping.

In my mind, I see an unfinished tapestry, honoring the era of the "Camelot" attributed to the beloved first family of that time—the Kennedys. Sadly, the tapestry will remain "unfinished" because someone so insignificant as this assassin dared to take down someone so significant to the nation and the world—our President John F. Kennedy. How unfortunate and unfair that we, as a nation, would never realize John F. Kennedy's full potential as our president and the leader of the free world! Eternal memory to you, Mr. President! The nation will never forget you nor the never-to-be-forgotten excerpt from your inaugural address: "Ask not what your country can do for you—ask what you can do for your country."

Our patriotic newfound friend—the cleaning man—packed up his tools, said a tearful good-bye to us, and went home to be with his family. Hand-in-hand, we crossed the threshold to our apartment and collapsed on a couch. With barely enough strength, we turned on the radio. We continued to hold on to each other as we listened to the news we wished—from the depth of our beings—had not happened.

For the next several days—following the assassination—the somber music on the radio resonated throughout our apartment. We half-listened and half-dried salty tears from our burning eyes. The time-defying epic hymns and songs that brought me peace and joy in the past, now portray sadness and grief.

"I Come to the Garden Alone"

"Amazing Grace"

"Nearer My God to Thee"

"Where Have All the Flowers Gone"

"Long, Long Ago"

How can I forget—along with others of my generation—that frozen moment in time, aired on every television station everywhere, when, in a blink of an eye, the joyous presidential entourage in Dallas changed to tragedy that stunned the world? The much admired first lady, Jackie, in her blood-stained pink suit and a pillbox hat crouching over her dying husband, helpless and stupefied? I can't! We shouldn't!

——-

Now to much happier times. Our baby girl arrived on December 15, 1963, several weeks too early. Her due date was the end of January. Although tiny—less than five pounds—to us she was the most beautiful baby ever born. I am sure we've all heard that story before from parents everywhere about their babies, especially the first-time parents like we happened to be at the time. My first glance at our baby girl was joy beyond anything I had ever experienced. To my eyes, she was perfect in every way and, of course, her elated daddy, grandparents, aunts, uncles, and cousins all agreed. Kyra—translated from Greek, means "Lord, have mercy," chosen by her adoring father—was the quietest baby in the hospital's nursery. While other babies cried and wanted to be changed and fed, our baby just slept as if she was still in the womb, where—in reality—she still belonged. The nurses brought her to me always fast asleep, and took her back to the nursery sleeping as well. I never fed or changed her during my five-day stay in the hospital. The nurses, however, assured me she was well taken care of, and praised her outstanding behavior in the nurs-ery. I know better today. Babies do cry because that's the way they communicate with their caretakers when they're hungry or need a dia-per change. But did I give it a thought that maybe there was a problem that wasn't being addressed? No!

I was a "mommy" of leisure during those five days in the hospital, free to enjoy the Christmas decorations from my maternity room's large window—and through the baby-wing of the hospital—overlooking the City of Elizabeth in all its holiday splendor. And I considered myself—in all respects—the happiest and most blessed person on earth. I even questioned my own happiness, because, at times, it seemed too good to be real or true. But it was, until we brought our baby, Kyra, home weighing eight ounces less than at birth.

My husband, John, practically sterilized our entire apartment before we brought our precious, sleepy baby home. There was no room for Kyra's crib except in our one and only bedroom, next to our bed, leaving hardly enough space to walk around the room. We both agreed, however, the lack of space for a nursery should not be a problem with a baby like our beautiful baby-doll daughter that never cried, at least not in our presence. In contradiction to our assumed reality, the very first night at home with our premature infant put our knowledge about babies to test we never expected or imagined—at least not so soon.

Being the youngest in our families, neither one of us had experience with taking care of babies, especially a tiny one like ours. Kyra had awakened as soon as we crossed the threshold to our apartment and cried through that entire first night. She refused the formula prescribed by the pediatrician altogether, and no rocking, burping, changing diapers delivered the comfort we wished for Kyra and for us—the exhausted, bewildered first-time parents.

We changed pediatricians and formulas, but nothing seemed to work. In desperation, our new pediatrician suggested a predigested formula which we needed to order especially for our baby through a special distributor—very expensive and time-consuming in preparation; six hours of slow cooking (after the powder was dissolved) in a special receptacle for a couple days of feeding. I have since forgotten the name of this concoction and perhaps for a good reason. But we were delighted we found something that seemed to work, so we could keep our sanity and watch our baby girl grow. But we were shocked—beyond words—when the pediatrician told us: "You have a baby with a severe colic, likes of which I had not seen in the past several years of my practice; and I suspect allergies as well. She will eventually outgrow the colic, of course, but it may take months."

Months? We both exclaimed at once and looked at each other in disbelief. We couldn't even imagine another week of endless sleepless nights and days. The upstairs and downstairs neighbors were driving us crazy by their knocks on the floor and the ceiling night after night, day after day. They were already testing our patience and frustration to the point that at times we felt justified in returning their rudeness, but we resisted the temptation because we realized the constant crying had to be annoying to them too. But shouldn't they at least try to be a little understanding? We questioned as the days, weeks, and months were passing.

We finally decided that the only way my husband can get a decent night's sleep and keep his job, was for us to move the crib to the living room and close the door to the bedroom where he slept. During the long sleepless nights and days that seemed without end, I comforted myself and Kyra, seemingly still in excruciating pain—but thank God thriving—with a promise that each passing painful day and night was bringing us closer to that magical time when we will enjoy each other because all three of us will be healthy, and sleep-deprivation will be a thing of the past and soon forgotten. And, maybe soon, we will have a home of our own and the knocks on the floor and the ceiling will disappear like snow in springtime. And if—on occasions—she'll feel like crying for whatever reason, or dancing in the arms of her devoted father and eventually atop his feet, all will be joyfully received because every inch of our home will belong to us. Sadly, tons and tons of muddy water had to pass under that invisible bridge before that promise would finally be realized.

We received forty some little dresses for our baby girl from well-wishers. Unfortunately, all were packed away untouched, because Kyra outgrew them before she outgrew her colic. Our hats are off to people/person who came up with today's baby registry. There were so many things we could have used for our first baby, but all we received were very cute but tiny dresses. Oh, well, such was the life back then and we were there.

With days getting longer, snow turning to puddles of water and crocuses—the first heralds of spring awakening from their long winter sleep—gracing the greening earth with their colorful blooms, our colicky baby began to smile and laugh aloud, and so did we. We outlived the colic and now we could all enjoy good nights' sleep and each other. So, we thought. But for us, the rainy season was not over.

I called my parents every day to check on them (as well as my mother-in-law), because all three of them were in failing health, especially my dear mother. But on this particular morning—completely out of character—my invalid father answered the telephone and in an effort to protect me, pretended that all was well at home, but my gut-feeling told me otherwise. When I pressed further—my distraught father—told me the truth. "Your mother is gravely ill and was taken to the Medical Center in Jersey City by ambulance early this morning. Please get there as soon as you can."

The shock to my system was too much. I dropped the telephone and left my helpless father hanging on. I grabbed a glass of water and ran back to the telephone. He was still there, seemingly frightened to death that something had happened to me and there was no one to take care of Kyra. I reassured him, the baby and I were both fine, and that I would meet him in the hospital. I made an emergency call to my husband in school.

We found my mother in an intensive care, suffering from a heart attack in addition to a possible metastasized cancer and Graves' disease. The diagnosis was devastating! Eventually, she was released from the hospital but, of course, never recovered. She was confined to bed and needed round-the-clock care. My life became one confusing mess. I felt as if my being suddenly split into two different parts. One desperately wanting to be with my dying mother, and the other with my husband and the baby at home. How could I satisfy both and, in the end, myself? I wondered. As spring turned to summer and the apartment became unbearably hot, I would pack Kyra in a baby carriage, which I had to retrieve from a dark corner in the basement—assigned to me by the stern landlady—holding Kyra close to my breast, because of mice and rats I occasionally spotted there, and trotted to Warinanco Park for a breath of cool, refreshing air. Those trips to Warinanco Park with Kyra—now decades later—still resonate sweet memories, except for the fact that my dear mother could never join me and watch Kyra sleeping peacefully under majestic trees, waving in gentle summer breezes—or playing on the wind-swept green grass, reminiscent of a plump, flower-strewn carpet. How I wished my mother was well enough to spend even one hour there with me and enjoy the baby in that lovely natural setting. But all my wishes, hopes (and even prayers) remained unfulfilled. Things were spiraling downward fast. And I made a decision—with my husband's approval—I never regretted. I temporarily moved—with Kyra—to Jersey City to be with my dying mother and invalid father. With help from my family living upstairs—my brother Michael, sister-in-law Justine, nephew Roman, nieces Luba, Myra, and Eugenia (I lovingly called Jeanie)—I managed to take care of my dying mother, and the baby, the last six or seven weeks of her life. She lived to see Kyra take her first steps at ten months. My beloved mother died on November 2, 1964 at age sixty-one. How blessed I was to have a loving husband and a precious baby who helped me through this difficult time and healing that followed.

In recalling the emotional rollercoaster decade when we lost our president to an assassin's bullet, I would be remiss if I failed to mention two more tragedies that befell our nation and the world during that troubled decade of the sixties. An American clergyman, activist, and prominent leader in the African-American civil rights movement, Rev. Martin Luther King, died from an assassin's bullet on April 4, 1968 at age thirty-nine in Memphis, Tennessee. Martin Luther King, Jr. Day was established as a U.S. national holiday in 1986. Dr. King's speech in Washington, D.C. in 1963, "I Have a Dream," gained national notoriety. Robert F. Kennedy, senator from New York, former attorney general, beloved brother of President John F. Kennedy, lost his life to an assassin's bullet on June 6, 1968, during a successful presidential primary in California. He was forty-three and father of eleven children. This was a decade of overwhelming turbulence which spared no mercy or compassion for people living at the time, and generations yet to be born.

# Chapter Nine
# A Break in the Clouds

The snow was piling up on the streets below, the windowpanes were rapidly changing from clear glass to frosty, glistening designs and our apartment—as usual—was following suit with the weather outside. The early occurrence of heavy snow for this time of year—the latter part of November—was not common, but not unusual. What was out of character—at this late hour of the evening—were the unexpected repetitive loud raps on our apartment door, which grudgingly interrupted our quiet time with our baby before bedtime. Who could this be at this late hour on a snowy evening? We wondered as we raced to the door not knowing what to expect—little Kyra in her daddy's arms for safety. For a brief moment, I dared to think that, perhaps, someone in our apartment building took time to read the notice—our thoughtful Avon lady had posted in the entrance hallway—about the recent passing of my dear mother and was here to express condolences and bring words of comfort. A gesture I would have gladly welcomed—and John too, for my sake— no matter how late the hour. I quickly dismissed that possibility when the overzealous landlady's face appeared in the doorway, an official looking brown envelope protruding from her hand.

"I know it's late but I need to talk to you right now," the self-serving landlady—accompanied by her husband—sputtered. Then without waiting for an invitation to come in, stepped over the threshold, her timid husband following in her footsteps, and began her recitation of tenant violations we had "supposedly" committed while living there.

"First offense," the landlady spewed. "I received complaints from the residents of this facility that an unattended baby carriage was left in the entrance hallway, which had to be yours, since you're the only couple in this building with a baby," she emphasized as if to remind us of that fact, brazenly pointing to sleepy baby Kyra in her father's arms, and continued to babble on. "I assigned you a place for the baby carriage in the corner of the basement where such things belong. By not obeying my orders, you have violated an important rule of the building code and that's a felony," she stressed and went on.

"Second important regulation—very important," she emphasized the word "important" and continued. "The clothes-drying lines in the courtyard are for my use only." You broke that rule when you hung some diapers there to dry one day. If this happens again, the diapers will be disposed of in the garbage receptacle in the basement, and not returned to you as I have graciously done when I saw them on one of the lines," she warned and jumped to the last offense without giving us a chance to respond.

"Third—and most critical misdemeanor—she sputtered, pulling out what looked like a bill from the same large brown envelope she brought with her. "You have flooded the kitchen floor below your apartment, and are responsible for the damages the water had caused. Here are the charges, so pay up as soon as possible, if you want to avoid trouble," she sternly stated while handing us the bill; we were not aware it existed. John looked at me quizzically and motioned for me to respond, since everything we were being accused of happened when he was at work, and I at home with the baby. To say that I was surprised at those unfounded accusations would be an understatement. I was fuming on the inside, but knew I had to collect my composure before I began the defense. I took a deep breath and let my feelings of injustice take over—unrestrained—come what may. I would begin by explaining to the landlady why I chose the particular solution to each problem that arose from living in an apartment not conducive to raising a baby. Surely, she would understand my situation of distress in each case. Especially, if she still remembered that she actually encouraged us to rent this third-floor apartment, when she knew about its shortcomings—rules and regulations—but never once mentioned them to us. Did she not remember—from her much younger days— that babies usually followed marriages, and we were a young married couple when she rented this particular apartment to us? I was anxious to get started, felt confident of vindication in every case, and certain that our life would continue—unchanged—until we decided otherwise sometime in the future, when we were ready for a home of our own.

"Let me begin at the beginning concerning the baby carriage. Yes, I left the carriage in the corner of the hallway on one occasion. My husband was due home from work any minute, and I knew it would be easier—and safer—for him to drag the carriage to the mice-and-rat-infested, wet basement than me struggling to get it there with a sick baby in my arms, returning from the pediatrician's office." This was the truth, but it didn't seem to have made a dent in the landlady's stern-looking face. I then proceeded to the next accusation, hoping for a sign of kindness.

"Yes, I admit to this outrageous felony—from your perspective— involving the two hand washed, wrung out diapers which one day, and only once, appeared on one of your clothes-lines in the courtyard for quicker drying, because I couldn't make the several blocks-long trip to the laundromat and needed a couple of dry diapers until my husband returned home from his job." I took another deep breath and continued. "You were still breathless from running up the three flights when you mercilessly began chastising me for this thoughtless act and threw the—still damp—diapers in my face. I realized you were the owner and we, the renters, so I apologized and gave you my word this would-n't happen again, and it hasn't. So, why are you bringing it up again and at this late hour?" I asked, looking straight into her stoic eyes. Still no response—good or bad—so, I moved on to addressing the last, and seemingly the most serious misdemeanor, while John listened, at first patiently, and minute by minute becoming more and more agitated by these unfounded accusations, and me desperately trying to make things right again between us and the landlord, obviously without success. The last accusation—flooding of the kitchen floor below us— made even less sense than the previous two. There was only one occasion—I remembered—that might have had something to do with water seeping to the floor below us, but nothing to do with my negligence. I would give it my best to explain.

"Let me refresh your memory about what you had told us about the unsightly, antiquated-looking tub in the kitchen when we rented the apartment. 'You'll find this gadget useful for rinsing out delicate hand washables.' That's exactly what I did one day. I soaked—for a couple of hours—our crisscross nylon curtains in the tub, towel-dried them, and hung them up. Water from the tub must have seeped through the broken pipes to the kitchen below. How else could the water have gotten there, if not by means of the broken pipes hiding in the wall?"

But the unrelenting landlady wasn't buying any of my sensible reasoning, and insisted we were still liable for the damages to the downstairs kitchen, because the damage occurred when we were living there. John and I looked at each other in disbelief and politely—but firmly—asked the unyielding landlady and her silent husband to leave, making sure the bogus hefty bill went with them. But there was something strange about this entire scenario that defied logic—we both agreed. Was there an underlying issue kept at bay from us for reasons unknown that was causing this unpleasant confrontation? Was something important being hidden from us? And, if so, why? We began to question and wonder. The minutes—and then hours—were ticking away and we all needed, especially baby Kyra, a good night's sleep nestled under the trusty featherbed blanket, with our little one in the middle, as usual, to keep her warm through the night. There was so much to think about and consider about what had just taken place, but it would have to wait until the three of us are well-rested.

The next day, the dependable Avon lady—one and only person in the building of thirty-some families we considered friendly—and a friend, who must have followed in my husband's footsteps because she appeared at our doorstep as soon as John returned home from his teaching job. She came without her Avon paraphernalia and seemingly on a mission that had nothing to do with selling her products. "I need to talk to you about something that involves you personally," she said with her head resting on her chest, as if whatever she had to tell us was too painful for her to disclose to us. She asked if she could sit down. Our curiosity piqued, and we—simultaneously—motioned to her to take any seat in the living room, our eyes fixed on her serious facial expression. What could be so urgent that couldn't wait another day or even an hour? We wondered with great concern. She asked for a glass of water which prolonged our anxiety. "I need to 'whet my whistle' before I can begin," she jokingly said, seemingly trying to alleviate the seriousness of the situation at hand, and approach the subject from a lighter side. The seconds ticked by and we were becoming more impatient and the baby increasingly fidgety. We wanted to hear—without further ado—what prompted this unexpected visit from the Avon lady. After another gulp of water she was ready to talk.

"The people in this apartment want you out, and soon. They are signing a petition. I am telling you this before you get a surprise eviction notice in your mailbox. This has nothing to do with you personally," she assured us and continued. "As you know, there are thirty-some families living in this complex and all are elderly. You are the only family with a baby, as you well know," the Avon lady paused for another sip of water and went on. "The residents in this building fear—especially the landlord—you will set a precedence for other families with children who might want to rent an apartment here and use you as an example, which would leave no room for the landlord to pull out, if she allows you to remain here."

The Avon lady's message of compassion—on our behalf—was appreciated but far from welcoming. Why didn't we see this coming? We wondered, reasoning that with Kyra's severe colic and my mother's passing, we overlooked the obvious. Now, the question before us! "How are we going to move—and where to—in the middle of winter with a small baby?" For us, the timing could not have been worse. We acknowledged and worried. Fortunately for us, our worry was over almost as soon as it had begun. The "worse timing" of yesterday suddenly turned to be the "right timing" a few days later—in this case. How true the saying, life is all about the right timing.

In the recent past, we had looked at some houses but not seriously. We never expected the unexpected that suddenly faced us. We thought we had all the time in the world to find that "one" special place we would both fall in love with at first sight, and help it grow into a real home, along with our growing family. But that's not the way real life works, we discovered sooner than we were ready to accept this reality. The unexpected hit us like a ton of bricks. Fortunately—

by the grace of God—life was on our side this time, as this "unexpected" turned into a gift that would keep on giving through the years.

Out of the blue, an adorable Cape Cod house—with plenty of room for expansion if needed—appeared on the market and happened to meet all our requirements. The house needed to be sold quickly to accommodate the owners' move to another state on a job transfer. There was little time for decision-making if we wanted the house. We were the first people to make an offer on this darling Cape, while others waited in line ready to jump in, if our offer was rejected. The wise realtor—we still fondly remember to this day—warned us of the fierce competition on this property, and suggested we bid above the asking price. We agreed! The expression "strike while the iron is hot" worked in our favor. Our impressive offer—and means to back it up—was accepted on the spot. Virtually, in minutes the deal was closed. Blessedly, the house of our dreams on the dead end street, spacious backyard enclosed by a white picket fence, in the lovely township of Cranford, New Jersey—where my husband taught school—was now ours. Cranford, referred to in one noted New Jersey magazine as "the Venice of New Jersey" because of its quaint beauty and the picturesque Rahway River conducive to canoeing. We could hardly believe how quickly it all happened. In the morning, we were house-hunters, and in the afternoon of the same day, we were the homeowners. Being in the right place at the right time was our "good luck," but we would rather refer to it—and remember it—as a "blessing from above!"

We wasted no time in giving written notice to the insensitive landlord—who wanted us out—of our intentions to move, before the eviction notice reached our mailbox. We were ready to say good-bye to apartment living when our month-to-month lease expired at the end of November 1964. Our priorities were now focused on packing our belongings, moving date, Kyra's first birthday, and Christmas—first of many to come—in our own home sweet home.

Winter came with a vengeance that first year in our new home. There was no denying, the job of digging out from layers of the packed white stuff—time after time—no matter how pretty and pristine it might have looked from the inside of our warm, comfortable home, proved daunting at times, but the memories we made that first winter remain priceless to this day. Especially, when we look at ourselves in pictures—as a young family frozen in time—frolicking in the snow, doing what needed to be done, while still enjoying our precious time together.

Kyra's first birthday party was one fabulous celebration in combination with the debut of our new home and observation of Christmas—opening its welcoming doors to family and friends from this day forward through the years. Our one-year-old daughter managed to shred open every gift she received, with no conception of value attached to any. But she sure enjoyed the applause after each successful unwrapping of every present: A string of cultured pearls from her paternal grandmother, Anastasia; a portable organ with sheet music by numbers from her maternal grandfather, John; a gold birthstone ring from her godmother, Aunt Eva (my husband's sister) with room for expansion as Kyra' s little fingers grew, and another one from her godfather, Uncle Nicky, and Aunt Irene (my husband's best friend); a miniature decorated Christmas tree from her Uncle Mike, Aunt Justine, and family (my brother and sister-in-law), boasting the Star of Bethlehem atop, fashioned from real money, a hefty bond from her Uncle John (my brother) in Cleveland, Ohio—not in attendance. The best was left for last as seen through Kyra's young eyes—a rocking horse from her Aunt Anna, Uncle Charlie, and family (my husband's sister and brother-in-law). Kyra was so entranced with her first life-like pony, that when it was time to blow out her one candle on the huge birthday cake and take some pictures of the occasion, she had to be physically removed from the rocking horse and tearfully carried to the table. Kyra's proud parents (John and I) opened a sizeable savings account on the occasion of her first birthday with a promise to add to it every succeeding birthday, which we faithfully followed. Kyra doesn't remember any of these precious moments of long ago, but we, her loving parents, do and question, "Where have all these years gone to?" All forty-nine of them as of this writing. How quickly—and stealthily—they have marched on into the future and eternity.

With holidays over—artificial Christmas tree taken down and stored in its permanent place in the basement-closet awaiting next unveiling, holiday decorations and lights boxed, labeled, and stored up in the attic—winter-blues started moving in on me and eventually succeeded in wearing me down. Kyra began exhibiting every possible symptom of ill health that puzzled even her pediatrician. What could be wrong with our adorable little girl? Why the constant high fevers and breathing problems? We questioned and worried. We thought the worst in raising a child was over when Kyra finally outgrew her colic, but that was not the case. But how were we to know the prime culprit that was making our child so sick were cigarettes, when smoking was so fashionable in those days and recommended even for pregnant women? And secondhand smoking was not even in the picture. Kyra was extremely allergic to smoke and my invalid father—a frequent long-term guest to our home since my mother's passing—was a chain smoker; Kyra's daddy also smoked but to a much lesser degree, but he gave up this addiction when Kyra was about two years old. Unfortunately, my father continued to smoke until cancer took his life at age seventy-seven. Years later, we learned how detrimental smoking—even secondhand—can be for people of all ages, especially those harboring other allergies like our child did. Over time, Kyra's health improved, thanks to years of immunotherapy treatments and "oodles" of painful injections.

My mourning for my mother remained unabated during those long, lonely snowed-in days of winter, alone in the house with a sickly baby—except for occasional visits from my invalid, grieving father—with no playmates for Kyra or friends for me in the new neighborhood that first deep-freeze winter. The web of grief seemed unrelenting and unbreakable. And then it happened! A dream—as real as life—of incomprehensible beauty, joy, and peace with my departed mother. The place she took me to was heavenly, so it must have been Heaven, and I was blessed to visit with her for those few precious moments that changed my life from overwhelming grief to divine peace, and blessed me with zest for living—once again—with my earthly family, where God wanted me to be, and where I was needed. The following account of my experience—with my mother—in the great beyond is true to the best of my unfailing memory to this day.

"Your continuing extreme mourning for me is making me very sad." I clearly heard those words in my mother's earthly voice. And there was more—much more. "If I show you where I am living now, will you promise me, you'll stop this absurdity and let me go in peace?" I remember embracing her and saying that I would do anything to make her happy, because I loved her very much. She then took my hand and—together—we were flying over picturesque lush green fields, dotted with varieties of brilliantly colored flowers. Blooming trees, outlandishly beautiful, lining the cobblestone roads, some resembling flowering magnolias in spring. The mind-boggling water-falls that seemed to have no beginnings or endings. The peace and tranquility I was experiencing in that other dimension with my moth-er couldn't compare to anything I had ever experienced—or imag-ined—here on earth. Suddenly—without a good-bye—a peck on my cheek and she was gone. But the experience of that visit with my departed, dear mother in that other dimension lives on…through the years, and serves to comfort—wherever possible—others, traveling this lonely road of bereavement. I make sure of that.

The days were now getting longer, snows were melting, snow-drops and crocuses were gracing the land with their smiling faces. Winter was over! Birds were singing again. Spring and new rebirth was back—and so was I.

# Chapter Ten
## Our Nest Is Blessed

As soon as the last snows of winter were gone, hunting for hidden spring treasures in our backyard—by the three of us—had begun. It didn't take long to convince us that spring was truly back and here to stay. A patch of yellow daffodils ready to unfurl their delicate pedals; spikes of fragrant purple, white, and pink hyacinths pushing through the moist soil towards the sun; buds of red and yellow tulips soon to dazzle our eyes with their cup-shaped smiling faces; several greening shrubs along the fence which—in due time—unveiled lovely pink and white roses; and round clusters of stunning rhododendron flowers, likes of which I had not seen before. And there were the three fledgling spruce trees bordering our property in the back, suggestive of a mini-forest suitable for nesting birds, which brought us even closer—in heart—to that living, breathing suburban atmosphere we craved in a home. Especially, after the many unhappy experiences we endured with our infant daughter while renting a third-floor apartment in the city. The memories we made that first spring in a home of our own will forever remain frozen in my mind, as one of the happiest times in my life on this side of the ocean. Regrettably, in the midst of everything spring-beautiful, an unexpected sadness gripped my heart again.

Two lilac trees (facing the back wall of the house) burst into eye-catching clusters of sweetly scented purple and white flowers. More marvels in our backyard to behold and rejoice, one would think, but not for me at the time. Lilacs were my mother's favorite spring flowers. Every spring, Mother would recall the happiness she derived from the lilacs she grew back in her homeland, and longed to duplicate this joy in her adopted country of America which—unfortunately—she never realized. And neither did my promise come to fruition when I constantly assured her she would have lilacs in her life, one way or another. I would make sure of that! But this was not to be because her destiny was more powerful than my meager earthly promise. Once again, I became immersed in an all-consuming grief and feared this debilitating emotional state was back to haunt me. Blessedly this time, the bout of sadness was short-lived, thanks to that extraordinary experience with my mother (reality to me) in that other dimension where beautiful flowers were blooming everywhere, where peace and joy reigned over everything, and spring appeared to be everlasting. To this day, I wonder! Was this phenomenon an actual out-of-body experience or some other divine intervention on my behalf? I will never know for certain. What I do know for sure is that, it brought me comfort and peace and led me to accepting what I could not change, and gradual emotional healing so I could live a full life again. I consider myself richly blessed to have had this—paranormal of sorts—never-to-be-forgotten experience. It has helped me through the years to better deal with other heartbreaking losses in my life, because, I believe with all my heart, there is more to life than our earthly existence and our eyes can see. If for no other reason than to offer comfort and peace to others, I would like to share my mother's last words to me: "I am not the first nor will I be the last. Please, let me go in peace. Don't mourn me more than you'll need to."

Every morning, we were awakened to the choruses of singing birds, and I heard their pleasant wake up calls loud and clear, again. The household chores were now done with ease and satisfaction—no longer the drudgery I was experiencing in the prior six months when my heart was heavy with grief. On weekends, we walked the neighboring streets with toddler Kyra in tow or in a stroller, enjoying different sights and picking up new ideas for our own home and grounds. We enjoyed looking at the impressive Victorian homes on the way to the Rahway River to show Kyra the ducks and geese swimming in the river. We visited—and revisited many times over—the Crane-Phillips House Living Museum, a small Victorian cottage that showed what life was like in the late nineteenth century, especially the "Kate's room," which had a dollhouse to teach Kyra to look but not touch. We took canoe rides with friends from Jersey City—our former home-town—and together we enjoyed our quaint town from the Rahway River view.

We collected buckets of unwanted dandelion flowers, growing in profusion on empty lots in the vicinity, for wine-making. This was my husband's pet project and it was successful for as long as he dabbled in it. Every Christmas, we gave out bottles of wine as gifts to family and friends. We planted a garden of tomatoes, cucumbers, beets, let-tuce, carrots—enough vegetables to share with the neighbors around us as well. That first year, our tomato plants grew so tall that my hus-band's picture appeared in the local newspaper with his gigantic toma-to plants, courtesy of the astonished neighbor who couldn't even grow weeds. The picture was captioned "Farmer John." Life was exciting and fulfilling, and became even more interesting once we discovered the Watchung Mountains, minutes from our home.

The expression, "You can take a boy out of the country, but you can't take the country out of the boy," typifies my love for the coun-try and the mountains. Our first outing to Watchung brought me to joy-ful tears. I could hardly believe this was reality and not a dream I would soon wake up from. My spirit soared as high as some of the tallest trees that seemed to be touching the blue sky above. How could this be? I marveled. We were so close to home and yet it seemed so far away from our suburban place! I had my mountains back without going back to my place of birth and childhood in my beloved Carpathian Mountains in another part of the world, and the place of my beginnings. How we enjoyed those nature walks with our little girl, and John never got tired—at least he never showed—of my ram-bling on and on about the mountains where I grew up. It was in the Watchung Mountains where Kyra first saw a real deer—reindeer to her—that helped Santa at Christmastime; a cottontail rabbit that brought colored eggs and candy at Easter; listened to the whispering pines and babbling brooks where tiny fish played; ran through the grassy fields gathering flowers for bouquets to give to her "overjoyed" parents—us. And it was to the Watchung Mountains we would "run" to get away from the day-to-day living and to regenerate for work-a-day routines. The closest Jersey Shore—at least an hour or so from home—presented more of a challenge for a quick getaway, but it was there for us to enjoy if we so desired. There is no denying, the state of New Jersey—known as the Garden State—is one of the smaller states in the Union of the united fifty states, but it has so much to offer. It has the mountains, the ocean, the lakes, the farms, the cities, the suburbia, the country. I feel blessed to be a part of it all.

To appease toddler Kyra constantly asking for a playmate, we adopted a darling, little calico kitten found in my father's backyard in Jersey City, seemingly unwanted, unloved, and in dire need of a loving home, kept alive through my father's—temporary—generosity on its behalf. This gesture on our part served everyone involved well. My father, because the responsibility for taking care of the little creature was becoming too taxing—being an invalid himself. Both of us (John and I), because we learned how to domesticate a stray, care for it, and give it love. Kyra, because she learned that love can be shared, and respect is crucial for all creatures.

We took the homeless kitten home and named it Pebbles because of its distinctive, pebble-like markings. Pebbles, the four-legged addition to our family, brought us joy and also challenges. No sooner did we leave the house—or even turned our heads—Pebbles would quickly seize the moment and challenge every piece of furniture in the house, the higher the better. She was full of life as well as mischief, which at times brought out the worst in us, but mostly the best that endeared her to us; and the longer she lived with us, the more we all loved her. But she was a feral cat, and no matter how hard we tried to keep her indoors, she would always outsmart us and find a way to freedom on the outside. She blessed us with three adorable kittens, before we had her spayed and took away her privilege to roam the neighborhood and get herself into trouble, again. Kyra, almost two years old, adored the two calico, like the mother, and one black—possibly like the father—kittens, and learned how to gently groom them once the mother, Pebbles, gained her trust. The kittens were eventually put up for adoption to the cat-loving families in the neighborhood, but it was very difficult to let them go in spite of the visiting rights we negotiated with the adoptive families. Pebbles was our first cat, but she would not be the last. She was merely the first of many "pussy cats" to be adopted and loved by us—a tradition that endeared itself to future members of our family, forever. Sadly, Pebbles met an untimely death—by a speeding car—when she disobeyed us and sneaked out one unfortunate night.

In reality, Pebbles broke the barrier that previously kept us closed off from loving all trainable animals and helping the unfortunate many who didn't have a fair chance in their innocent lives, (except snakes, because of one frightening experience, which I noted in my *Blossoms on a Rooftop* memoir in Chapter 13). I would be remiss if I didn't give due credit to our last kitty cat named Pepper. Pepper was a runt of the litter brought to us by the cat-loving neighborhood children. "Please take this kitty, because no one else will. We already tried every other family in the neighborhood," they pleaded. We reluctantly relented to their pleas and adopted this flea-ridden, abandoned by its mother, tiny—also deaf, we later discovered—creature. We nursed it back to health, had it spayed, kept up with necessary shots, and reaped the benefits of unconditional love for the next nineteen years. The more love you give to your pets, the more will come back to you—that's a promise from Pepper and all her predecessors we had the pleasure of having in our family over the many years.

As spring turned to summer and outdoor living became the norm, one by one, we met the neighbors on our dead end street and made lasting friendships with some. Kyra was growing by leaps and bounds and friends became plentiful on this family-oriented block. One day, a mother brought her two little boys to play in our backyard, and then another mother came knocking on the door with a little boy in tow asking if our daughter would play with him. She now had three playmates, and this was the beginning of "play days" until she started early kindergarten at age four and a half. How fortunate that, through our little daughter's friends, I made new friends as well—friendships worth their weight in gold. No more lonely winters for me and Kyra, again. Life was good and became even better when we received the best news of all from our gynecologist, Dr. Whitken, the following spring.

*We* were pregnant with our second child and couldn't be happier!

Note the well-deserved pronoun "we." My husband, John, graduated from Columbia University in New York City with a Master's Degree in Art Education, eventually earning thirty more credits to further enhance his chosen profession. Our nest was truly being blessed!

# Chapter Eleven
## The Greatest Treasure

Even the joys of a magical spring of that memorable year of 1966, could have compared to the joy in our hearts upon learning of the blessed event on the way, which would bring a sibling to our three-year-old daughter—when the baby came—and make us a family of four. The gender of the baby was not important to any of us. All we wanted, and prayed for, was another baby—God willing, healthy—to love, enjoy, and watch grow along with our firstborn little girl.

Our world of all blue sky became tinged with clouds of gray when the family doctor (also gynecologist in those days) warned of possible complications ahead with our second child. The culprit was the Rh factor (Rhesus factor) in our blood types—an incompatibility when an Rh+ man fathers a *second* child and subsequent children with an Rh-mother—which was our situation; usually bypassing the first birth, like it did in the case of our firstborn, who was not affected by the condition. How lucky we are today that this—potentially life-threatening problem for babies falling into this category—no longer exists, thanks to new discoveries in medical fields.

An injection of "antibodies" serum administered around the twenty-eighth week of pregnancy and again within seventy-two hours after the delivery of an Rh+ baby—for the first and all subsequent pregnancies—is all the present mothers need to undergo to avoid complications due to Rh factor blood incompatibility. Forty-some years ago, we were simply told by the compassionate family doctor/gynecologist to count our blessings if our second baby was born healthy and, respectfully but firmly, cautioned against a third child. The news was not what we expected or wanted to hear, but it wasn't the worst, we agreed after the initial shock. Our main concern was now focused on the wellbeing of our second baby-to-be. The doctor let us listen to the baby's heartbeat and new hope—as strong as the baby's heartbeat—filled our hearts once again. And his recommendation to limit our family to two children suddenly found its proper perspective. Why harbor resentments and disappointments about something not yet conceived, and may never be?

We faithfully kept up with visits to the laboratory for biweekly blood tests and visits to doctor's office to discuss the results and receive updates on the baby's progress in the womb. The first three months of the pregnancy were no different from my first, and I looked forward to the next —and last—six months to follow suit. But life is not always as straight forward as we would like it to be, or wish, it could be. In addition to the possible problems with our second baby, I was harboring health problems of my own, which I chose to keep to myself for fear of any intervention that might further jeopardize the well-being of the baby I was carrying. At times, the pain in my chest was so severe that—on occasions—it would bring me to tears. And the further I got into the pregnancy, the more excruciating—and more frequent—the pain in my chest became. Yet, deep down in my heart, I knew this was all about my distress and not the baby's. I just needed to stay strong and not give in to the sharp pains caused by the baby's kicking in my chest. Especially, at night when I tried to sleep, creating sleepless nights and floor walking, waiting for the dawn to break. You see, I had a hiatal hernia which I didn't know about and neither did the doctor. It is a protrusion of part of the stomach upward into the chest cavity—the source of my suffering in addition to burning acid reflux into my esophagus.

Fortunately, I was a stay-at-home mom at the time, so I slept when both of my babies were resting. One in the womb and the other next to me in bed—behind the locked bedroom door for safety—caressing her favorite teddy bear, sipping juice from her "sippie" cup, until sleep won over her wide-open, big, blue eyes. And sleep always won over, every afternoon for two or three hours. And if she had awaken before I did, there were her favorite toys scattered around the room to keep her entertained. As the sayings go: "Necessity is the mother of invention," and "desperate times call for desperate measures." The time of sleepless nights was now nearing the end and I was "mighty" glad, even though I didn't know what was waiting ahead. But who among us mortals does?

November 27, 1966—three days after Thanksgiving—our precious baby girl joined our family. By the grace of God—except for moderate anemia and significant jaundice—she was perfect, full term, and weighing 7 lbs. 2 oz. For precautionary measures, I was told later, she was placed in an incubator which worried me to death, since our first daughter (premature) weighing less than 5 lbs. was not incubated. Hours later, which seemed like an eternity, I was allowed to hold our "bundle of joy" for the first time, count the fingers on her little hands and toes on her wrinkled feet (don't all mothers do that?), and show her off to her beaming daddy. How unfair that fathers were not allowed in the delivery room back then. Five days later, we brought our treasure home and introduced her to big sister Kyra, let her hold her future "forever best friend," while we, their proud parents, enjoyed this once-in-a-lifetime precious moment, and documented it by taking a few pictures. We were now a complete family with two great daughters and a playful—at times mischievous—much loved kitty cat named Pebbles. We couldn't stop smiling and thanking the good Lord for our two greatest treasures on earth. But there was one terrifying moment at the hospital while we were waiting to take our precious baby home. For about ten minutes —an eternity for us—our baby was missing from the nursery and no one knew where she was. Panic! The nurses began scurrying from room to room looking for her while we were—literally—dying on the inside. She was finally found in an unoccupied room at the end of the maternity floor, being prepared for going home by a nursing student unaware of the hospital protocol. We were too numb to demand an explanation or an apology. All was well because it ended well and we were on our way home.

The honor of naming our second daughter was bestowed on me,

since Kyra's daddy had the pleasure of naming her. John chose the name from a short liturgical prayer that begins with, or consists of the words "Lord, have mercy"—transliteration of Greek *"kyrie eleison"*—and the middle name after his oldest sister Ann; combination of the two resulting in the name of Kyra Ann. I chose a name from my favorite soap opera—long gone from television—"Another World." The name Laura means a "crown of glory"—for us a glorious gift that would forever keep on giving. I named our daughter after a lovely young woman playing the role of a doctor on the daytime serial drama, who won my admiration for her dedication to healing others. And the middle name after my youngest niece, Eugenia, I lovingly nicknamed Jeanie or Jean—that's how our second daughter became Laura Jean.

The words from the concerned doctor, "Your baby isn't doing well," touched us where it hurt most—in our hearts. The latest blood test showed the anemia was not going away and the weight was at a standstill. The concerned Dr. Whitken suggested Vitamin B-12 injections and supplemental feedings. Of course, we agreed. The heaviness from our hearts was slowly being lifted when the injections and supplemental feedings began showing signs of improvement. By six months, we were almost out of the woods. Kyra still remembers dancing around and making funny faces at every feeding to distract her sister, while I (we)—literally—shoved little bits of food into Laura's mouth, making sure she properly swallowed it and not begin chocking or spitting food out, as she often did. We practically force-fed Laura Jean that first year of her fragile life. Seeing our baby girl thrive was all we needed to continue our efforts in earnest and be grateful for the rewards. I would gladly do it over again if I had the chance.

I kept Laura in a bassinet next to our bed for the first six or seven months, until I felt comfortable I didn't have to nudge her at night to start breathing. It seemed I always woke up (or did I even sleep?) just in time. Was this a sign of the SIDS syndrome (sudden infant death) or a result of a secondhand smoking? How well I remember my dear father and loving grandfather—a chain smoker and a frequent guest to our home—holding the baby with one hand and puffing on a cigarette with the other. It didn't take long, on every visit, for the entire interior of the house to be overtaken by swiftly traveling fog of smoke and offensive odor we were all breathing in, especially our young children with breathing problems. Were some of these breathing problems due to secondhand smoking? Probably, but who knew? Little was known back then about SIDS, or the hazards of smoking, and secondhand smoking was not even considered.

Barely two months old, baby Laura came down with her first "croup"—episodes of difficulty in breathing and hoarse metallic cough—that plagued her for the next five years. Even moderate wind outside would make her gasp for air. I spent more nights over her crib, and then a child's bed, than I spent in bed sleeping next to my husband. And the vaporizer ran nonstop every night during those frequent attacks, the vapor actually stripping the paint to bare walls in the room. One winter, we lived through ten attacks. Many times, in the middle of the night, we ran hot water in the bathtub to create enough steam and keep Laura in there until her breathing became less labored, but my vigil continued through each night. Often in the wee hours of the morning during those episodes, my body craved sleep so badly, but my maternal instinct told me otherwise, and I always listened. I remember an elderly aunt stopping by one day, who assured me that time will come when I would wish for less sleep. But, of course, I didn't see this time coming any time soon—or ever. "Easy for you to talk, now that you have all the time in the world to sleep as long as you want, and whenever you feel like sleeping." I politely reminded her.

# Chapter Twelve
# Growing and Learning Together

The anticipation of starting kindergarten in the morning made for a restless and sleepless night for our four-and-a-half-year-old daughter, Kyra, and for the rest of us in the household as well. Several times during that night, she awakened us asking the same question: "How much longer until morning and time for school?" Was Kyra that excited about starting school or was there a hidden element of fear in her anxiousness she was not telling us about? Was our child even ready to begin kindergarten? We grew concerned and questioned. Being born at the end of the year, she would be the youngest in her class, and with no older siblings at home to model after, we anticipated some separation anxiety, but never to the extent Kyra would soon exhibit. If her birthday had come just two weeks closer to her due date—she arrived seven weeks too early—one more year at home, exposed to children her age outside of school, might have made all the difference in her readiness; but her December birthday mandated that she'd be enrolled for kindergarten and we abided by the rule, which would soon come back to haunt us.

Kindergarten for our little daughter was the first structured learning experience, as well as discipline dictated by a stranger everybody called Mrs. "F," and not Mommy and Daddy she was used to at home.

How unfortunate there was no preschool that we were aware of when Kyra and her younger sister were growing up, forty-some years ago. In those days, the first introduction to school for the little ones was the kindergarten. How lucky the preschoolers—as well as their parents—are today to be exposed to so many learning media at an early age, such as preschool (or nursery school), visits to libraries, trips to the malls, restaurants, playgrounds, parks, grocery stores because transportation is much more readily available, especially if the family owns two cars and both parents are able to drive. We had only one car and I didn't drive—not unusual for women of my day.

Finally, the morning of the first day of school for our anxious child had arrived! The first sign of morning light brought Kyra to her feet and to our bedroom, the new green dress—her paternal grandmother bought for her especially for this day—on her arm, and the black patent shoes and white socks in her hand. "It's morning, time for school!" She declared, loud enough to wake everybody up. Not even the promise of her favorite breakfast of pancakes drizzled with maple syrup excited her more than school. "I am not too hungry today. I just want to get dressed and go to school." She emphatically informed us. We lovingly embraced her, looked into her eyes and told her about the schedule we would follow on school days.

"When we get up in the morning, we say a short prayer that you already know; we prepare breakfast and eat together at the table; after breakfast we brush our teeth; we then get dressed and leave for school." She seemed to understand—and slowed down a bit—what was required of her and of all of us for this schedule to work. After all was accomplished, her daddy took some memorable pictures of his little girl as she was closing the door of her safe home with one hand, and smiling, waving good-bye to us with the other hand while clutching to a small mat—required by the kindergarten class—to rest upon during the fifteen-minute nap times (with lights off).

Kyra was too young to know she was not only waving good-bye to us, but also to carefree childhood days that were abruptly ending. She was too young to know, she was stepping into a brand new world of learning and responsibility that would continue throughout the rest of her life. Her daddy gave her a tender hug and a kiss and—with misty eyes—left for his own teaching job, no doubt, to face other parents bringing their little ones to school for the first time and finding it hard to let go of the small trembling hands clenching to theirs for dear life. School girl Kyra and toddler Laura—in the stroller—smiled all the way to school, and both girls were as happy as the singing birds in the cloudless, blue sky above on that long-ago, September day in 1968. They didn't realize—and neither did I—this joy would end the moment we reached the school and the time for us to leave Kyra.

The kindergarten teacher was waiting at the door, welcoming her new, first-time students. When Kyra's turn came she unclenched her hand from mine, and motioned for me to leave. While this direct approach might have worked with the other kindergartners, it didn't work with ours. In fact it frightened her half to death. She began screaming at the top of her lungs, broke away from the teacher, grabbed the corner of my skirt and her sister's hand in the stroller—who was now crying uncontrollably as well—and refused to let go. I could only imagine how terrified she must have felt. Under normal circumstances, Kyra was a happy, friendly child, ready to befriend anybody who would smile at her (not a good thing in today's world). Not this time! No amount of my pleading—and a promise we would soon be back to pick her up and bring her home—would persuade her to join the other children in the colorfully decorated classroom. Finally, the teacher took the reins into her own hands. She bodily picked Kyra up, told us to go home, and disappeared behind the closed door with my screaming—obviously very frightened—child.

Looking back today, I question. Would it not have been better for all concerned to let us stay in the classroom—two people Kyra knew well and loved—that first half-day of school to help her in the transition from all-home to mornings in school? Knowing what I know now, that's exactly what I would have insisted upon today. Instead, I went home distraught with guilt, fighting back relentless echoes in my head of my little girl's desperate cries. At home, I questioned myself—should I go back to school and pull my traumatized child out of the classroom? Regrettably, forty-some years ago when we were young parents, suggesting alternative ways—or questioning anything about our children's schooling—was frowned upon, not only by the teaching staff, but also by other parents (except in extreme cases), and we abided by the belief that educators knew best how to educate our children and what was best for them (and in most cases this was true then and still is today). But so did the parents know then and still today.

Suddenly, out of the blue, the familiar trusting voice in my head made its presence known and claimed my attention as it always did when I was at the crossroads. I relaxed and listened. "Don't pull the child out of the classroom. Put on a happy face when you pick her up from school at noon. Tell her how proud you are of her. Embrace her not with sadness but with gladness. And don't be discouraged if this recipe is not an instant success. Give it time to work and patience to see it through. Remember, all good things are worth waiting for!" My maternal instincts validated these valuable suggestions and I followed them in earnest. Time passed and I felt comfortable telling Kyra's concerned daddy our little girl was adjusting well to school and we were on the road to success. I spoke too soon!

With only a dozen or so half-days in kindergarten to Kyra's credit, she decided the school was not for her and made this stunning announcement to us at suppertime one evening. "I want to quit school." She told us boldly. "I don't like anything there. The teacher is mean! She keeps putting me in the 'thinking chair' every day and lets other children play. I am not going back there again! I want to stay at home and play with Laura and Pebbles." Puzzled, John and I looked at each other lost for words. What do you say to a kindergartner that wants to quit school?

"Let's ask her if she knows why Mrs. F has her sitting in that dreaded thinking chair every day, hear what she has to say and go forward from there." I suggested. It worked!

"I am put in the thinking chair every time I cry and don't listen to Mrs. F when she asks me to stop." Kyra readily revealed. The next logical question was to ask why she cries so much in class. She had the ready answer for us again. "I miss you and I don't want to be in school without you." She promptly answered, watching our faces for reactions.

"Okay, we can fix that." I assured her. John gave me a quizzical look and motioned for me to start talking. "You know that daddy has to go to work to teach other children, but Laura and I can be there, but in another room—only steps away from your classroom—and can even wave to you through the glass window every day."

Kyra's face lit up and her eyes widened. "You can do that?" She asked while jumping up and down, throwing kisses in our direction.

John looked at me disapprovingly and asked, "Are you for real or is this some kind of a joke?"

"I am for real, trust me," I assured him. "The school is looking for volunteers to help in the library, I can bring Laura with me, donate my time and be there for Kyra at the same time—in another room but in the same building, as I promised, and wave to her now and then too."

John smiled and replied, "This will work. Do it!"

The time, I donated to the library paid off a hundredfold in hundreds of ways for all of us as well as for the school. First and foremost, I helped Kyra in her difficult adjustment to school; exposed toddler Laura to groups of children visiting the library with their teachers, including her big sister's kindergarten class. I smiled—admittedly with a twinge of sadness—when Kyra first came to the library with her class and didn't run to me or her sister next to me, quietly flipping the pages of a picture book. She just waved and gave us a great big smile, as if to say. "I am a big girl now! I don't cry in class anymore and don't sit in a 'thinking chair' every day. I listen to my teacher and not only to my mommy and daddy, and play with other children and not only with my little sister at home." It seemed our homebound little girl changed to a school girl overnight.

My work in the library was well-received and appreciated which made for a great reward in itself, in addition to the benefits our own two children derived from my volunteering in the same school until our younger daughter started kindergarten, blessedly well-prepared for school, and our first daughter successfully moving on. The expression, "love conquers all" bears witness to its truth and so do I.

Our girls were growing and learning and we were too. John and I attended evening classes for adults in local high schools, year after year. Sewing, crocheting, knitting, and embroidery piqued my interest. John's fervor rested in art, such as scenery painting and portraiture, eventually leading to specialized study of iconography and painting—referred to as writing, taught by the masters of this art. Writing of Holy Icons of saints is revered by the Eastern Orthodox Church and its people; he successfully completed many beautiful ones and gifted them to the family for posterity.

I followed my passion for sewing, knitting, crocheting, and embroidery. I made identical dresses for the girls, dresses for me, curtains and drapes for the windows, and even slip covers for couches. I knitted and crocheted sweaters for John and the girls, colorful afghans, hats, mittens, scarves, embroidered couch pillows for displays, and pictures for special family occasions such as birth announcements, wedding mementos, and house blessings. You name it and I made it and enjoyed doing it. But that was then when my eyes were young, and so was I.

Gardening brought pleasure to both of us, but especially to John, so I usually just enjoyed the fruits of his labor in exchange for home-cooked meals and clean house. The few fruit-bearing trees in our backyard blessed us with abundance of delicious fruit in their seasons. Enough peaches to enjoy through the season, for preserving in glass jars for winter, and for sharing. Golden—sweet like honey—plums that ripened all at once, and most of them had to be given away because their shelf-life was so brief; oh, but how we enjoyed their blossoms in springtime. Abundance of red currants John took pride in turning into delicious jams for the family. Raspberry bushes that yielded enough fruit for us to enjoy in cereal through the season. A grape arbor with clusters of sweet, purple grapes suitable for wine-making, but we simply just enjoyed what we could and gave the rest away. A fig tree that gave us delicious figs in the fall, when most other fruit in our backyard was long gone. And I must not forget to mention our impressive vegetable garden, every year boasting plump, red tomatoes in its season, cucumbers, beets, carrots, parsley, and celery for soups—some of which we dried to be used in winter. We utilized every inch of the ground in our backyard and took great pleasure in watching everything grow, bloom, and produce fruit of its kind.

Life was good and rewards were many! Our girls were doing very well in school and we were bathing in their scholastic accomplishments. Then, out of the blue and for no immediately known good reason, our motivated first-grader, Laura, stopped bringing homework home or beginner-reader books from the school library she so loved until recently. And then, the unanticipated progress report from her teacher that shocked us. "Laura doesn't know her alphabet and is unable to sound out the words as a result. She needs special outside help. I need to meet with you, ASAP."

The program, called ITA, or Initial Teaching Alphabet, was recently introduced to Cranford's lower elementary schools on trial basis sometime in the late 1960s or early 1970s, in hopes of creating better readers through symbols representing letters of the regular alphabet used in a context of conversational spelling, stood out as possible culprit affecting our child's learning. To add credence to our suspicion, we recalled receiving information about a new reading program to be tested on students in our children's school. The meeting with the newly hired first-grade teacher, who replaced the retiring in mid-term ailing teacher, confirmed our suspicion. Our daughter didn't know the regular alphabet and couldn't read, because she was never transferred from the unconventional stuff consisting of symbols.

Dad and mom to the rescue! We took it upon ourselves to learn the unprecedented alphabet and its use, taught it to our perplexed child, transferred her to regular alphabet—not addressed by the retiring ailing teacher—and helped her through the transition period and beyond, until we felt her confidence was back, and strong enough to meet the challenges in school on her own. Our efforts paid more than we bargained for. Her next progress report outshone our expectations by far, which—in reality—became our little girl's foundation to a scholastic success that followed her throughout all the years of her schooling. Our older daughter, a fourth grader, was already a good reader when the ITA program was introduced to the school, and she breezed through this new system of becoming a quicker and more proficient reader without our help; but, oh, how grateful we are today that our vigilance generated such unforgettable benefits—gifts that will continue to keep on giving throughout all the years for all of us, but especially Laura. This pilot project lasted only two or three years in our school and faded away, remembered only by those students and their parents who lived through it, our family notwithstanding.

In 1976, our township of Cranford celebrated the 200th anniversary of its founding, and the children of Cranford schools—including high school—were invited to participate in the bicentennial logo design contest. We can proudly affirm that our eleven-year-old daughter Kyra's design—sixth grader at the time—won the first prize, and her third-grade sister Laura's composition about the township's special celebration of the occasion, also expressing the pride in her big sister's achievement, was chosen to accompany the design in a capsule buried on the grounds of the Municipal Building—together with numerous other important memorabilia and items depicting life in Cranford as it was one hundred years ago—to be unearthed and opened in one hundred years. One hundred years is an eternity for us mortals, but it will be a testament of proof long after we're gone, that we once walked these streets, celebrated good times and mourned the sad ones. Kyra was presented an award of recognition by then Miss New Jersey, and the picture of the presentation appeared on the first page of the local newspapers. Her design holds the honor of distinction in a composite of important historical landmarks in Cranford, displayed in public buildings to this day. Our girls contributed to Cranford's history and have blessed us with forever pride.

Those were good times for us and our family. We saved enough money to purchase a second secondhand car. I learned to drive so I didn't have to depend solely on my husband to take me and the girls everywhere. It took some time for me to be comfortable behind the wheel, but I persevered and, eventually, reaped the benefits of independence and freedom, which benefited our whole family. With the car at my disposal, I was no longer housebound when John was at work. My whole world opened up. I was now able to drive the girls to school in inclement weather—otherwise they walked the half mile or so distance. I could also shop for groceries by myself, which freed John from constantly going with me. I enjoyed going to town with the girls just to walk around and look at the window displays, or have a leisurely lunch for just "us girls." I seriously question today, how did I ever get along without driving? And why did I wait so long to get my driver's license?

# Chapter Thirteen
## Memory-Maker Moments

We all have memories we wish we could throw away and forget, and memories we want to hold on to and remember forever. Memories of special events in our lives that changed our lives, such as a marriage, a birth of a child, or a new job for instance. But there are also those subtle memory-maker moments in our day-to-day busy lives that are simply just tossed aside and, in time, erased from our minds and forgotten as if they never happened—that is if we let this happen. I consider myself fortunate that I had recorded some of those precious moments in my life along with frozen in time, priceless photos that continue to bless me with smiles when I need them most. Blessings of "smiles," I pray, which transcend time and space on the way to you, dear readers, and prompt you to look for your own trove of treasured memories—we all have them—to bring you "smiles" on cloudy days, and to sustain you until the sun shines for you again.

The sleepless nights for us—especially for me—finally ended! Our girls were now sleeping through the nights and so were we. We survived the colic, childhood-related diseases, health problems challenges, difficult beginnings in school, defining moments of teenage years and beyond, and lived to tell about the lessons we had learned from this memorable journey—laden with happiness and, sometimes, tears. But the tears were in time forgotten but not the rewards—those remain unforgettable. Who could forget the heart-warming, innocently humorous stories children bring home from school, especially the beginners? Let me cite a few examples our little ones shared with us.

One evening at suppertime, Kyra—now a seasoned kindergartner—shared this delightful story with us: "I am beginning to like school. Today, I raised my hand in class and answered a question no one in my kindergarten class knew the answer to, except me," she boasted. We prompted her to go on. "Mrs. F asked if anyone in class knew who Neil Armstrong and Buzz Aldrin were, and I knew." John and I looked at each other in amazement. We knew our child was smart (all doting parents and grandparents attest to that fact), but not this smart! How did Kyra know about the first American astronauts who landed on the moon on July 20, 1969? We questioned each other, when subjects of that complexity were not discussed with our young children. Still, we were impressed and wanted to hear more. Truth be told, she didn't really know. When pressed for an answer, this is what she told us: "I told the class that Neil and Buzz were our milkmen" (note the first name basis here).

Incidentally, can you imagine having milk delivered to your doorsteps today? We did in those days—twice a week at dawn—but definitely not by the Messrs. Armstrong and Aldrin, the national space heroes. Sorry about that, gentlemen (Astronaut Neil Armstrong died on August 25, 2012). We tried to put the spilled milk back into the bottle but found it impossible, so we chose the second best in this case. We explained to our youngster the difference between an astronaut's job and that of a milkman. "Both very important," we told her, "but as different from one another, as earth is from the moon, and the moon from the nearest star." The illustration on paper helped, and Kyra was ready to take the next shuttle to the moon. But since this was not possible anytime soon, it at least sparked her interest in space travel.

"Mr. Armstrong and Mr. Aldrin were never our milkmen, my dad and mom said I should tell everybody. They were the first American men who flew to the moon," she told everyone in class the next day, "and never anybody's milkmen," and then added this, she told us at supper table that evening. "I thought if I raised my hand and answered a question," she spilled to the class, "Mrs. F would let me leave the dreaded thinking chair, but all she did was smile and told me to ask my parents about those two men, and I did, end of story." And check this doozy credited to Kyra.

"Mommy and Daddy, are you awake?"

"I am now," I groggily answered. "What's the matter honey?" I asked, but didn't wait for Kyra to respond. "I'll be right there!" I assured her, stumbling to my feet and rushing to her bedside, before the rest of the household awakened, especially my husband who had to be in school—well rested and bright-eyed—in just a few hours. "What's wrong, sweetheart? Do you feel sick?" I anxiously checked for fever by placing my hand on her forehead and felt, somewhat, relieved there seemed to be no evidence of high fever she was known to run. But I remained concerned until Kyra assured me.

"Don't worry, Mommy, I am not sick. I just want to ask you something very important," she murmured.

"It's two o'clock, after midnight; couldn't this 'something' wait until the morning?" I could have guessed her answer.

"No, Mommy, because I am awake now and remember the question now too." Against my better judgment I gave in to her explanation on the condition that she would make the question short and sweet. She nodded her head. "I know everything there is to know about sex and want to know if you and Daddy ever had it in your life."

I froze! My first impulse was to scream for my husband to wake up and help me deal with this startling question, but I quickly changed my mind. A question of that intensity from a young child at that ungodly hour of the night, would only create more chaos and confusion. I decided to deal with it myself as best I could, and speak to the kindergarten teacher about this incident when I dropped Kyra off in school in the morning. Meanwhile, I opted for the simplest answer I could think of—"Yes," I answered, and bit my lips in expectation of a detailed explanation. To my surprise, there was none, unusual for this inquisitive child of ours. She gave me a kiss and a hug, said goodnight, whispered "Thank you, Mommy," closed her eyes, and fell into a sound sleep before I even left her room—never to raise the question again. Sometimes, the simplest answer to a complex question works best!

We never did pursue this issue further, because we felt there was no need to do so, until several years later when Kyra was old enough to understand, needed to know about such things and Mother Nature validated the timing. Times have changed and safety concerns for our children have changed too. How sad for the parents and children growing up in today's world when we teach them not to speak to strangers—run away from people they don't know who want to befriend them, and holler for help. The analogy "it takes a village to raise a child" has, unfortunately, lost its sentiment of truth, and the trust we believed in when we were raising our children decades ago, no longer exists. How great it would be if we could turn back the clock to the simpler times of yesteryears—at least where our innocent children are concerned—when a handshake meant a contract and "it took a village to raise a child," figuratively speaking. Children are reflections of their nurturers and mentors. Let us give them what they deserve and need most. The best of ourselves, as our first daughter gave to us when she was a child on a class trip.

The miniature pitcher and saucer, still displayed on a window sill of the family room in our home, will forever remind us of the moment in time when Kyra spent her lunch money to buy this treasure for us on a fifth grade class trip. On the way home, in all her excitement, she dropped this "treasure" and the whole thing shattered into pieces. She collected the fragments and, devastated by the loss, brought them home, bitter tears flowing down her cheeks. To help her overcome this trauma, we took her back to the place where she purchased this priceless gift—as soon as it was possible—and she bought an exact replica from the savings in her piggy bank and joyfully presented it to us. Not to leave her younger sister out, she whispered in her ear, "The gift is yours too, Laura." How could we ever forget this precious moment? Not in this lifetime!

Toddler Laura outgrew her toddlerhood much too soon for our liking, skipped from grade to grade almost in a race to catch up to her older sister in school, or so it seemed. She was now the one bringing home entertaining stories from school, but most endearing were her first cursive-writing compositions from the third grade when she was eight years old. Below are a few examples of how she saw us—her parents—at that tender age in her life when we meant the whole world to her. I had the description of her father framed and Laura gave it to her proud daddy as a gift for Father's Day that year. I received mine the following Valentine's Day—the framing courtesy of my husband.

My volunteer work in the library starting from Laura's toddlerhood until she began kindergarten paid off in ways that couldn't be measured in dollars and cents. The children's picture books of different animals, landscapes, farms, trees, oceans, flowers…. I entertained her with while working as a librarian, spurred in her the appreciation and love for all nature, forever. She learned early how to take advantage of the library's lending system and used it to the maximum. There was always a different book she would bring home, even before she could actually read: Books on farm animals—especially horses, wild flowers, mountains, kittens, cats, dogs…and for me, she would lovingly bring the *Ideals* magazines, featuring stunning photography of nature and inspiring stories I loved to read, and still do today.

My husband, John, was the arts and crafts director for our township of Cranford's summer playgrounds program for most years of our girls' childhood. They traveled with him from one playground to the next, summer after summer, until they outgrew the interest and age limit. Over the years, we collected enough arts and crafts to fill an attic. Few boxes still remain—labeled and checked from time to time—and like other treasured memories from days gone by, we continue to hold on to them, and probably will for as long as our home remains "ours." Does the metaphor "one person's trash is another person's treasure" bring to mind the memory of something that means the world to you, but only to you and nobody else? And that's what memory-maker moments are all about in my view. Not to live in the past but remember the best of it.

# The Man

The man is huge and handsome and nice and tremendous and gigantic and powerful and great and mighty and cute and tall. But he is not bulky and wide and broad. But do you know who he is? He has a beautiful wife. He is my father!

Kyra's miniature saucer and pitcher that made history.

# My Mother

My mother is the beautifulest mother in the whole Universe! I love her! She is sweet, kind, and nothing can top her! I love my mother!!! ......

"The Lady in my Life"
Laura
2-6-73

"The Lady in my Life" is my mother. She takes care of me when I'm sick. And when I'm sad she cheers me up. And I love my mother.

# Chapter Fourteen
# The Best of Times

The expressions "to each his own" and "different strokes for different folks," may not necessarily appear to complement each other when viewed separately and hurriedly, but when examined closer and in combination, both clichés communicate the same persuasion: We are all unique individuals, different from everyone else by way of ideas, personality, and character ingrained in our distinct DNA. For the same reason, happiness is not "one size fits all" phenomenon. We search for our own sense of happiness—that special feeling that makes us feel good, secure, vibrant, and fulfilled—and we know when we have found it. I've found that missing link to happiness when I married my longtime high school friend—stealthily turned sweetheart—John, then twice more in my adult life when our daughters, Kyra and Laura, were born and made us a complete family unit.

Watching our children grow, growing and learning along with them, were the best years of my life by far and—I believe—of John's as well. Those unforgettable times when every day was a different experience—seldom anticipated—and never boring or trying, because the challenges made life exciting for us all. Take, for instance, our summer vacations—the last two weeks in August every year—when John's summer work on the playgrounds ended, and schools remained in recess until after the Labor Day weekend. Those cherished days will forever remain as my shining-star-moments in life.

Our motor trips took us to every eastern state in the union—from the tip of sunny Florida to the tip of nature-endowed Maine; plane trips—and rental cars—to western states of this marvelous country of ours. And what "mine" eyes (ours) have seen there, defies any imagination or realm of possibility in the mind of the first-time visitor. Let me take you to some of these awe-inspiring places that left indelible impressions on our minds, hearts, and souls, as well as gratefulness for the privilege of seeing for ourselves how magnificent this land of ours called America truly is.

One of the greatest wonders of the world, in my humble opinion, has to be the Grand Canyon National Park in Arizona. There is no way to describe this miracle of nature—and do it justice—without seeing it with one's own eyes, and that's what I wish for you, dear reader, if possible. And there were other mind-boggling wonders of nature we were privileged to be a part of as well: The picturesque Big Sur region of California; the Golden Gate Bridge; the "golden" hills of San Francisco and the cable cars we rode on; the breathtaking Yosemite National Park, and the world-famous Yellowstone National Park in Wyoming, where animals roam freely and the view extends as far as the eyes can see.

The excitement of mapping our trips, pinpointing places of historical interests we wanted to see; making reservations for hotels/motels with pools along the way; stopping at scenic rest places for picnics; the ratings assigned to each overnight stay according to girls' fervors, starting at "0" to number "10," made every trip fun and gratifying beyond any measure. Most places we stayed at over the years received high marks, only one motel failed to rise to the occasion and received a big fat "0" on all counts, and for valid reasons as you will see.

Traveling through the state of Georgia, enjoying the pastoral country scenes, we lost ourselves in its uniqueness and didn't realize the daylight was quickly fading away and darkness was fast approaching. We traveled several additional miles through pitch-black, winding country roads, praying to find a place to spend the night before we wound up in some unseen, dark ravine, no exit way, or someone's private property. Finally, a flashing "VACANCY" sign appeared off the less-traveled country road that uplifted our spirits. With a sigh of relief, we followed the bright arrows to the motel, looking forward to a restful night in clean, comfortable beds. To our horror, the room we were led to by a maidservant was beyond the meaning of "unaccept-able." It was, literally, a disaster area, reeking with offensive odors, especially from the bathroom littered with unsightly paper and towels; bathroom was the one place we always checked first before settling down for the night in any hotel/motel during our travels. When we went back to the so called "office" and asked for a refund, the person behind the desk refused to return our money. The maidservant followed us out. Reluctantly, she whispered in my ear, "Someone in that room committed suicide the night before and the police traffic, to and from the room, kept me from giving it a thorough cleaning." And since this forsaken unit was the only vacancy on the premises, she offered to help us out. "Give me an hour or so of your time and I will have the room cleaned—spick and span—from top to bottom," she promised. But we decided we'd rather spend the night in our car than go back to that morose room, knowing what had taken place in there only hours earlier. With the owner's permission, we traded the deposit on the room for a parking space on his property and let it go at that. We were safe for the night and that's what mattered. The saying "all's well that ends well" happened to be our case, the unexpected silver lining to this one-of-a-kind story.

At the first sign of daybreak and wakeup rooster-crows all around, we got back on the road and stopped at the first luncheonette where early rising farmers were gathering for breakfast and to discuss farming matters, as it turned out. What a treat and unexpected rewards—to boot—stemmed from this unfortunate experience. The delicious breakfast of grits, bacon, eggs, hash brown potatoes, toast, unlimited cups of freshly brewed coffee with homemade fruit pies for desserts, and the valuable lessons we learned about farming, more than made up for the inconvenience—and on some level hardship—we encountered earlier. The farmers were talking among each other but loud enough for us to hear and we listened intently, because theirs was another way of making a living—and making us well fed and happy—we, city and suburban folks, knew little about or paid much attention to. To put it bluntly, we took for granted. We learned how different weather pat-

terns affect different crops; the fluctuating market prices for fresh produce and where to sell it for more profitable income needed in its pro-
duction; where to buy best seeds and farm equipment, most reasonably
for next growing season…and all this information straight from the
farmers' themselves—or to put it in the vernacular, straight from the
"horse's mouth"—which broadened our knowledge about farming and
appreciation for country living. No one asked what we were doing
there at that early hour of the morning but the waitresses' welcoming
smiles, farmers' friendly glances, and their parting words—"You all
come back again, will you?"—said it all. The sleepless night in the car
no longer mattered, but the desperate individual who took his/her life
evoked our sympathy and prayers for some time to come. Every vacation was a special adventure. I only wish there had been more of
them—lot more, and that our girls took their time growing up so we
could enjoy them together. But that's not the way real life goes.

How well I still remember—when our older daughter reached the
age of fourteen—praying for time to slow down, and for God to grant
us many more years of summer travels as a family; continue to revel
in our girls' accomplishments in different areas of school life, especially in academics; watching them play their flutes in marching
bands, at football games, instrumental concerts in school; listening to
their piano concertos and other music—not always easy on the ears—
resonating from their shared study/bedroom on the second floor, at
times loud enough to bring the house down. And there were long summer days at Cranford community swimming pools—two of them to
choose from—when the girls challenged their father, each other or
friends in swimming races, followed by steaming hot pizza lunches,
hot pretzels, hotdogs, and cold drinks; playing games in the shade or
snoozing in the sun dreaming sweet dreams. And I must not forget to
mention our trips to the Jersey Shore, frolicking in the billowing ocean
waves and long walks on the beach, collecting shells and watching different boats whizzing by over the rolling waters. Or our Sunday afternoon rides after church to the mountains or outings to the country in
spring, when apple trees were in bloom, and in the fall when apples
were ready for picking and to enjoy the dazzling foliage displays, followed by meals out afterwards. Everything I, unfortunately, missed in
my growing up years when times were different. But, in reality, noth-

ing had really been lost for me, because I lived to see my children enjoy the opportunities I wasn't privileged to have, and that joy made up for all I might have missed with my parents and siblings, so, I harbor no resentments or regrets today, and don't take for granted the happiness I've found through my own family. Life is too short—and too precious—to waste on resentments or regrets. It's better to count the blessings instead. And, I hope, you will find enough blessings to count in your life, as I have found in mine, to keep us both busy and happy.

Kyra, our first born, was in the second half of her junior year in high school when we began looking for colleges in her chosen profession, which happened to be pharmacy. We traveled to different states, enjoyed the trips, and visited various pharmaceutical establishments, finally settling on one in-state school, the Rutgers University School of Pharmacy in Piscataway, New Jersey. Kyra's senior year in high school flew by faster than birds on wings in our own backyard, followed by her younger sister's senior year which passed just as fast. Graduations from high school came and went, and reality of colleges—for both of them—took root.

John and I checked our finances including our combined incomes—and what we had saved for the girls' education over the years—and realized it would not be enough to put them through five years of school required for certifications. I loved my part-time job in Cranford public schools as teacher's aide, but we both agreed the time had come for me to get a full-time job and bring home more income. I decided to go back to school for brush up courses in secretarial field, which was my work before I became a mother, and was soon employed in same capacity by a Fortune 500 company known at the time as American Home Products from which—years later—I retired, concurrently with John's early retirement from school in 1992 due to his failing health, and the division I worked for became sold. How grateful and proud I am today that I was able to help our girls attain their dreams—and our dreams for them as well—for good education which led them to "good" professions in health fields: Kyra as a pharmacist and Laura as an occupational therapist.

We were all overwhelmed with sadness when the day to move Kyra to her new residence in school suddenly arrived, and the reality of her leaving home—perhaps for good—faced us head on. I couldn't imagine our home without her. Not even when she and her younger sister, Laura, argued about things I wasn't privileged to know, which was quite often. And when I tried to help settle the arguments—whatever they were about—their reply was always the same: "Leave us alone, we're sisters and sisters are suppose to argue and sometimes fight too." And my reply to them was always the same too: "Just don't kill each other, you two!" But in spite of their frequent sisterly spats, and sometimes playful fights, I knew deep down in my heart how very much they loved each other and how much high school freshman Laura, at the time, would miss her big sister she looked up to and admired. She showed it when the telephone rang at a certain time every evening and she would jump to be the first to answer in hopes that it would be Kyra calling, and mom and dad didn't use up the allotted time on the payphone Kyra was using before she had her chance to talk. Or when we planned on visiting Kyra in school—packed with homemade goodies—Laura was always ready to go, even offering to take Pepper, our kitty cat, with her to cheer her sister up. Kyra shared her room with two other roommates, but Pepper would unfailingly choose her bed to sleep upon and bypass the other two, as if she knew which bed belonged to Kyra. Pepper would cuddle up in the handmade (by me) afghan, like she used to at home, and sleep peacefully until it was time for us to leave. And she never failed to plant a kiss on Kyra's cheek before bidding her goodbye, and lovingly handed over to Laura to be taken home.

Too soon, Laura reached the status of the second half of her junior year in high school, and the search for the "right" college started over again. She applied to several out-of-state universities and one in-state school. Lo and behold, she was accepted to every one of them. Now the dilemma: which school would be best for her chosen field of study, which happened to be occupational therapy? We were delighted that—after much deliberation—she chose the Kean University in Union, New Jersey, which was within commuting distance from home. We will never know for sure if she chose the nearby school for fear that, if she moved to another state, she would miss us—her parents—too much, or her devoted kitty cat, Pepper. Pepper followed Laura everywhere in the house—almost as if she was afraid that, without her watchful eye, Laura would leave her like her other adoring sister did.

Pepper studied with Laura night after night without a "meow" of complaint. You couldn't ask for a better roommate and friend who loved Laura unconditionally—no different from her mom and dad and older sister, Kyra.

It seemed like only yesterday when our girls were babies, suffering from all sorts of childhood diseases and other troubling health problems, and I thought they would never grow up and let me sleep through the night undisturbed. Now that they were mature, college graduate young ladies, holding prestigious jobs, earning their own money, driving their own cars, and I could sleep through the night, I wished I could turn back the clock to those cherished years when our lives were intertwined with theirs and revolved around them most of the time. How strange that we don't always fully appreciate what we have until we no longer have it. But that's human nature and par for the course, I suppose. But it's worth remembering that grass is not always greener on the other side of the fence as it may appear from a distance and, also, that all stages of our precious children's lives are cherished moments, worthy of tucking into the banks of our memories.

# Chapter Fifteen
# The Empty Nesters

The season of spring is that delightful time of year when we celebrate the rebirth of nature and all its glory. It is the time when the freeze-ravaged, crusty white earth miraculously changes to a kaleidoscope of shimmering colors to dazzle our winter-weary eyes, and renews our winter-depleted spirit with new enthusiasm and vigor for life. Spring is the time when our much-loved feathered friends return from their wintering warmer places in the south to our northern backyards, meadows, and forests and fill our silent days once again with their cheerful singing. And it is during this glorious season that our dexterous songsters build their unique nests for next generations of their species, lovingly take care of their broods until they are ready to fend for themselves and strong enough to fly on their own, and let them go to follow their destinies—just as human parents do. This phenomenon of nature is one unchangeable constant that makes our world what it is, keeps everything on earth in check, and makes life interesting and rewarding, despite occasional sadness and tears.

The handwriting on the wall was crystal clear that our firstborn daughter was ready to leave the safety of the nest we built for her and her sister, when she dropped all her other dates in favor of one young man, and her eyes lit up like stars on a dark night when she spoke of him, received long-stemmed roses from him "just because," as Kyra would say with a twinkle in her eyes that said more than she cared to share with us.

One day, almost out of the blue, the young man we suspected of winning Kyra's heart came down on one knee before her surprised father, a small blue velvet box in one hand and starry-eyed Kyra's hand in the other, asking for her hand in marriage and for our parental blessings—a traditional marriage proposal passed down from generations past we grew up with, and now sweet recollections of our own engagement twenty-seven years ago. Suddenly the "someday moment" John and I talked about from time to time, became the "now moment" when our first child would be getting married. And it all happened so quickly, almost in a blink of an eye, so it seemed when that time was here. Years have a way of slipping away from us quicker than we would like to see them go!

Soon after the bestowal of our blessings upon the young couple, and the beautiful gold-diamond ring—crafted by Kyra's now fiancé, Christopher Michalski, a jeweler residing in Canada—was placed on her finger, the plans for the wedding took root. And since the long-distance relationship was becoming too difficult for both of them, we all agreed. Several months later, on March 11, 1989, Kyra and Christopher were married in a beautiful traditional—rich in symbolism—Eastern Orthodox Church ceremony, followed by an elaborate wedding reception for about 250 guests. After a two-week honeymoon in Hawaii, Kyra packed her belongings in her car and followed her husband in his car to Montreal, Canada, their new home, where our new son-in-law had his jewelry business and Kyra planned on studying French at the—all-speaking French—University of Montreal, take her Pharmaceutical Boards in French, and practice pharmacy in dual languages. John and I worried she was overextending her efforts in this—seemingly all-consuming—decision and secretly questioned her overzealous enthusiasm. But to young Kyra, this was merely another challenge she was ready to face head-on and conquer. And she did accomplish what she set out to do! She successfully passed her board exams in French and was soon employed by a French/English speaking hospital in Montreal. She reached her goal and sounded happy each time we spoke to her on the telephone with herself and her new way of life. Then one day she broke down and confessed, "My job is challenging and fulfilling and I am happy speaking in two languages, but I miss everybody back home more than I ever thought it would be possible." It appeared that it was easier for Kyra to learn a foreign language than to learn to live without her family and friends.

Laura and I were at work when Kyra left for her new home in Canada with her new husband, so we were spared the painful good-byes. It all fell on Kyra's father who happened to have a day off from school and was at home at the time. He opened up to us at suppertime that evening, tears still trickling down his cheeks. "I never thought it would be so hard to let my little girl go and for her to leave the only home and family she ever knew, even if it was with a man she loves." He dried his tears and continued. "It hit me like a ton of bricks when I realized my little girl will be living so far away from her family and friends, tread uncharted waters in a country so different from her own." He rested his head on the table and started sobbing again. A minute or so later, he picked up his head, dried his tears, and went on. "When we finally let go of each other and I thought the good-byes were over, lo and behold, Kyra ran back to embrace me once more and kiss my hands again." If this wasn't enough for me and Laura to bear, my visibly shaken husband and daughters' protective father, told of his emotional state following Kyra's actual departure. "Once Kyra turned the corner and was gone, I completely lost it. I not only cried, I wailed," he confessed, his face ashen and swollen. It was time to put things into perspective and I took it upon myself to do it.

I pulled the three of us into an embrace and spoke from the depth of my heart, "I know Kyra didn't leave home because she stopped loving us or we stopped loving her and told her to move out. We all know this is furthest from the truth! She left of her own choice and because she fell in love with a young man of her choice. She left because she was ready to fly on her own—just like the nestlings in our backyard from their nests their feathered parents built for them. And we loved her enough to let her go and blessed her new married life. Let's be happy for her and not grieve as if we would never see her again." Then I added, "Let's plan a weekend trip to Canada as soon as the newlyweds are settled and ready for company."

"What a great idea. I am ready to go any time," my husband cheerfully responded and Laura validated the idea, her clapping echoing throughout the house. Our tears were replaced by reassuring smiles, and we eagerly waited for the telephone to ring, wishing it would be Kyra telling us they arrived safely. Our wishes came true, almost instantaneously.

"All's well! It was a very long trip and we're tired but happy to finally be at home. By the way, when are you coming to visit?" Kyra chimed and Christopher echoed from behind, "Come soon!"

I turned to my husband and whispered in his ear, "You see, we didn't lose a daughter, we gained a son-in-law." And then I whispered in Laura's ear, "You didn't lose a sister, you gained a brother-in-law. Remember my precious, your sister will always be your sister and best friend, no matter how great the distance between you, because love transcends time and space and that bond between you—as well as all of us—will never be broken."

We treasured the time we continued to have with Laura still at home, but again, the writing on the wall was clear our time together under the same roof was dwindling. History tends to repeat itself and Laura soon followed in her big sister's footsteps. We suspected things were getting serious between Laura and the blue-eyed, tall young man, Jonathan Dobias, she met where they both worked. Laura was already an occupational therapist and Jonathan a physical therapist, when she stopped dating other young men and devoted herself solely to Jonathan. Then one day, shortly before Christmas—three years after her sister's engagement—Laura came home with her now fiancé, Jonathan, flashing a beautiful gold and diamond engagement ring. Jonathan chose the peaceful Watchung Mountains setting for their momentous moment. He asked Laura's father for her hand in marriage when they came home—beaming with love and joy. Their beautiful wedding on October 9, 1993, with an elaborate reception also for about 250 guests, was almost a replica of her sister's wedding, per the young couple's wishes and their parents'—on both sides—blessings.

Following a two-week honeymoon to Tahiti, the young couple moved to an apartment complex in a neighboring town, so there were no tearful good-byes like with our first daughter—thank God. We were now officially empty nesters and wondered where have all the years gone to? The first two stanzas of the following lyrics by Harry

Belafonte, Alan Greene, and Malvina Reynolds from "Turn Around,"
a 1964 classic oldie, expresses our feelings best and resonates, I am
sure, with other parents as well:

> *Where are you going*
> *My little one, little one*
> *Where are you going*
> *My baby, my own*
> *Turn around and you're two*
> *Turn around and you're four*
> *Turn around and you're a young girl*
> *Going out of the door*
>
> ———
>
> *Where are you going*
> *My little one, little one*
> *Dresses and petticoats*
> *Where have they gone*
> *Turn around and you're grown*
> *Turn round and you're a young wife*
> *With babes of your own*

Even our kitty cat, Pepper, (Laura's roommate and faithful friend)
felt the emptiness when Laura moved out to her new apartment with
her husband. In an effort to let us know that Laura was missing from
her room/bedroom for several nights following the wedding, Pepper
kept on running up the stairs and down to where we were sleeping,
crying in her loudest meows yet, seemingly alerting us that Laura was
not there. How strange that she never did that when Laura was away
on trips or vacations. She sensed this absence was different from all
the others in the past. And some still say animals lack feelings and
even abuse these innocent God's creatures! One night, we followed
Pepper upstairs, took her into our arms, brought her downstairs, and
put her in bed with us, and that was where she slept from then on,
peacefully. And she always cuddled up on Laura's lap when she visited. Pepper's love for her sister, and former roommate, never wavered

and neither did Laura's for Pepper.

With our girls on their own, it was now our time to enjoy, together! We decided to retrace our wedding trip to Virginia in an effort to recapture some of the excitement and joy of those first days of our marriage thirty-one years ago. This was a nice, relaxing trip, but to say that it met our expectations of yesteryears would be an overstatement. The places we then stayed at were no longer there, on their sites residential complexes or newer and larger guest accommodations stood. The family eateries we so enjoyed then were also nowhere to be found, replaced by modern franchises popular up North as well. But we found it refreshing to reminisce about the "good old days" while making plans for future trips to places we had not visited before—trips for the two of us, alone.

Our cruise to Bermuda was first to any island via water or plane, and it was something new and exhilarating for both of us to experience. We loved the tour around Bermuda's capital of Hamilton and its old English-style churches and buildings; the schools of fish in the ocean—clearly visible through the "glass-bottom boat"—piqued our special interest and deemed repeated excursions. But my favorite— besides the spectacular ice sculptures, delectable dinners, and buffets—was an introduction to slot machines while the ship zipped through the open ocean waters. My downfall was the "beginner's luck" of winning two jackpots which hooked me for the entire cruise. Upon our return to the mainland, I tried my luck in a casino—two hours away from our home—in Atlantic City, New Jersey, but my luck was seldom repeated. Nonetheless, John and I took pleasure in this newfound diversion and enjoyed our day-excursions for several years. It was refreshing to walk on the boardwalk by the ocean—barred only by the inclement weather—followed by a fabulous, leisurely buffet and a little excitement playing slot machines with quarters set aside for this purpose. At the end of five or six hours there, we were ready for the return trip home and sleep in our own bed, some time with few extra dollars in our pocket, and some time with empty pockets, but always happy to be home and looking forward to the next monthly outing. Those were happy days I will remember forever—sitting next to my husband on the bus, holding hands, watching the scenery passing by with not a care in the world. This was our time together!

Our next trip and last big one was a three-week journey to my native homeland in the Carpathian Mountains, Lemkovyna in July of 1999—where I was born and lived until the age of fourteen. For John, this was his first visit to the place of his predecessors and his connection to the land he only heard about from his parents, where their roots were and, subsequently, John's, as well. There was much to explain to my bewildered husband about the history of now forgotten, forlorn land where, for generations—still clear in my memory, homes stood and families lived; children were born, people died and were put to rest in the now overgrown, neglected church cemeteries. We found many family names on the tombstones in John's parents' village of Zyndranowa, as well as in mine in the village of Leszczyny. John was amazed that I still remembered where each house stood and who lived there, even though the places were now obliterated by the passage of many decades of time and overgrowth.

I desperately wanted to show my husband the places where I spent my youth tending the cattle, as well as some secret places I played in during the long days in the pasture fields, always being mindful of the herd in my care, and watching the slow-moving sun over the vast sky until it reached the far horizon and time for me to lead our three milking cows home and collect their milk. This all changed when Derek, a young cousin who showed us through the village, grabbed my hand and literally flung me to the side when I tried to pull up blades of tall grasses from around the base of the monument by the roadside of our (once) property, say a little prayer, and place a handful of wild flowers, which I used to do as a child when thanking the Almighty God for His blessings upon our family and land, a tradition I learned from my mother. Wrapped around the base of the monument were two huge—probably poisonous—snakes John and I did not see, but Derek, with his young, trained eyes, did. Thank you **Lord** for placing Derek where he most needed at this crucial time.

The rest of our trip to the land of my beginnings was spent in the lovely resort town of Krynica—still in the Carpathian Mountains—as well as with Derek's family in the village of Losie just over the mountains, grateful to be alive, away from the snakes and wilderness. The cliché "you can't go home again" will forever ring true in my mind, but not in my heart and soul, because I need only to think about my ancestral village in the peaceful Carpathian Mountains, and I am there. But not the way I found it on my return trip, but the way I remember it—full of life and blooming meadows. That's the blessing of memories! We returned safely to our "home sweet home" and our loved ones in America, thankful for the experience, enriched by special memories and pictures to share with our loved ones in "the land of the free and the home of the brave!" (Check Operation Vistula or Akcja Wisla about "Lemkos" forced resettlement, if interested).

# From Our Wedding Albums

*Luba and John (10/6/62)*

*L to R:*
*Lillian Kopetz, Nick Motichka; bride &*
*groom; Eva Fedash; Vladimir Kopetz;*
*Sitting: Dorothy & John Phillips.*

*Luba and parents: John & Tekla*

*My parents' wedding:*
*Tekla and John (circa 1922)*

*Groom's family - Back row L to R:*
*Eva Fedash; Mom Anastasia; bride*
*& groom; John's sister Anna &*
*Husband Charles: Bottom row L to R:*
*Gregory; Michael; Deborah & Mark.*

*John's parents' wedding (late 1920's)*
*Anastasia and Michael Fedash*

*Kyra and Christopher (3/11/89)*

*Luba and brother John*

*Laura and Jonathan (10/9/1993)*

# Chapter Sixteen
# Beyond Imagination...

The Industrial Revolution was the period in history from 1750 to 1850 during which changes in agriculture, manufacturing, mining, and transportation began shifting from manually operated processes to power-driven machinery. It initially started in the United Kingdom, then subsequently spread throughout Western Europe, North America, Japan, and eventually to the rest of the world. It profoundly affected the social, economic, and cultural conditions of our early forefathers, and changed the ways they farmed their unyielding land, communicated with the rest of the world, and traveled outside of their simply constructed log cabins, built from hand-hewed logs and through hard manual labor. But there was more—much more—to this epic power phenomenon than our predecessors' limited vision of the world, and especially of its future, could have foreseen and their self-contained minds could have comprehended. And even more than the soothsayers' crystal balls—at the time—could have foreseen, because the full potential of the power discovery was hidden from the eyes of the world for decades to come; revealed only gradually and measurably to the world at large, until the plateau of today's achievement had been reached and full utilization attained. For now!

Our predecessors, most likely, couldn't even have conceptualized something as dynamic as cyberspace travel and electronic communication to every corner of the world, virtually within seconds, because the terms: cyberspace, Internet, or computer networks were not even in their rudimentary dictionaries when the Industrial Revolution initially rooted itself deep into the ground previously untouched by progress.

As today's senior, at times, I feel like the legendary character, Rip Van Winkle (circa 1819) in Washington Irving's *The Sketch Book of Geoffrey Crayon,* who slept for twenty years while the world of progress marched on…I wonder how many seniors of my generation—born in early 1930s—relate to my sentiments? Just curious! Even though—I assure you—I did not sleep anywhere near that formidable time. In fact, for years, I have suffered, and still do, from chronic insomnia problems and seldom sleep through the night. Most nights, I read until the wee hours of the night and fall asleep when the dawn is about to break and birds in the trees outside my window are beginning to chirp, which, for me, is not a wakeup call, but rather a sweet lullaby which lulls me to sleep for two or three hours, and I compensate for the rest through an occasional catnap during the day. A fringe benefit of long-awaited, well-deserved retirement!

Growing up in electricity-deprived mountain village during the Second World War, I thought the moon's purpose—high up in the heavenly sphere—was to supply us with light on dark nights, and the sun's daily traverse through the vast expanse of the sky was to light up the days, so people would know when to get up and start working in the fields. And for me to free our three cows from their tight stalls in the barn and lead them to green pasture fields, far away from home, interspersed with babbling brooks, pine and spruce trees, and wild flowers of every hue, especially the humble dandelions, which were encouraged to grow and thrive and not discriminated against, like they are in today's sculptured lawns, because the cattle loved them. And I innocently believed both entities—the moon and the sun—as well as the stars, belonged to the heavens where God's angels lived, and never a human foot to be set upon.

My childish conceptions of all heavenly bodies were wrong on at least one count. I was blessed to witness a miracle in the making and certainly "beyond imagination" when our first brave astronauts—Neil Armstrong and Buzz Aldrin—landed on the moon in July of 1969, planted our esteemed American flag on its surface, and left their footprints there for posterity. Today, there is even an international space station! How did we get to this point so quickly? And it all happened in my lifetime! God only knows where this rapidly expanding technology will take the next few generations after us. Without a doubt, much farther "beyond imagination..." for us living on this earth today, judging how far we've come in the realm of technology in the twentieth century and the dawn of the twenty-first century, respectively.

So often in the recent past, I would say a silent prayer for strangers walking next to me on the sidewalk in town or in the grocery store aisles, seemingly oblivious to everything—and everybody around them, talking and laughing to themselves, and ignoring all others in their path. At times, I even questioned why, suddenly, people have become so unfriendly and uncaring. What was really happening to our world? Then, one day, I realized the—self-communicating—strangers' ears were plugged up and they were actually carrying on legitimate conversations with other folks on the other side of the gizmos in their ears. And they were not suffering from some deep-seeded emotional problems as I erroneously assumed and needlessly worried there was something seriously wrong with all those unfortunate souls—and their numbers were seemingly increasing daily. *How very sad,* I thought to myself! And I wondered how we could help them as a society, and me personally.

I, too, carry a cell phone in my pocket and charge it on regular basis, but seldom find the need to use it in public and my number remains private. I keep it strictly for emergencies when I am away from home, but make all my calls in the privacy and comfort of my house and at my leisure. And that's how I like my private telephone conversations to remain, and business ones as well. But I must admit, it's nice to have that piece of technological marvel—the cell phone— near me at all times, especially when I am away from home without my caring and concerned husband, because it brings peace of mind to both of us that I am not really alone, which is reason enough to be grateful for its presence in our busy, global world.

I also have a computer but am not connected to the Internet, not yet. I use it specifically for word processing and find it indispensible in my writing. Without it, this book might not have been written, or, at best, remained a "work in progress" along with my *Blossoms on a Rooftop* in print for several years—with positive feedback from countless interested readers. Truth be told, when I was initially introduced to computers on my job twenty-some years ago, I secretly questioned its practicality and application to my job—and even resented its intrusion on my comfortable life in the workplace—when I was so proficient on my electric typewriter (a step up from the manual one I learned to type on), typing around 100 words per minute and never glancing at the keyboard. Today, I can't imagine myself without a computer—the spell-check feature on it, the ease of revisions, moving the text from one place to another without having to retype the entire document; or my battery-operated, trusty, pocket-size dictionary, which replaced the bulky, outdated, voluminous printed one, now doomed to eternal rest on a basement shelf along with other obsolete paraphernalia, awaiting their timely demise. This is an affirmation that we can adapt to different environments, conquer new challenges, and enjoy the rewards if we but distance ourselves from complacency and comfort zone that keep us from trying new things. But I, honestly, do not see the need—in my later years—for e-mail, texting, Twitter, or Facebook, among other "cyber" space stuff I am not familiar with, and don't wish to spend the rest of my precious years on earth learning about it for the sake of progress, when I can very well get along without these additional modes of communication for the time being. My voicemail telephone serves me fine for now. Thank you! Why on earth would I want to clutter my life with more unwarranted paperwork and responsibility when my daily mail is more than enough to sort through? And I enjoy writing personal notes on pretty stationery paper, and don't mind paying "our" bills via the trusty US post office. That's just my take on these things from my senior perspective today. Tomorrow may be a different scenario because my curiosity will, sooner or later, get the best of me and convince me that learning and trying new technologies is a challenge that defies age. And as a true "Taurus", according to astrological signs, I welcome challenges and thrive by them. So, don't be surprised if one day soon, you will be receiving an e-mail from me or a text message.

It was only recently when "our" concerned daughters graciously offered to equip our car with a gizmo called the GPS—Global Positioning System—or navigational system satellite signals, it was explained to us. We graciously thanked them but adamantly refused the offer, claiming our limited driving did not warrant such high tech equipment in our aging car. Shortly after—as luck would have it—I happened to be driving on a busy highway at traffic time at dusk, and mistakenly took a wrong turn on the way home. I was alone and soon desperately lost. I stopped at several gasoline stations and asked for directions to my hometown of Cranford, and people politely offered help. Unfortunately, the more directions I received, the less I knew where I was. It took more than two hours before I found my way home, when it should have taken less than half an hour. My husband John, was terrified that something awful had happened to me, and so was I especially since I left my cell phone at home. We know exactly what we want—as well as need—for the next gift-giving occasion. I commend today's seniors who are keeping up with those swiftly changing times and—I hope to stay afloat along with them—encourage and urge, our young people, the future leaders of tomorrow's complex world, to leave no stones unturned in search of new, fast-moving forward technology in all fields so they are well prepared for the winding roads and detours ahead. I wish you all Godspeed in this pursuit!

Regrettably, as I see it today, it appears that more specialties we allow into our already busy lives, the less time we have for things that really matter—whatever they happen to be in each individual case. And I feel disenchanted when I am told that something I value dearly—and still in good condition—has outlived its usefulness and considered obsolete, because the replacement parts, even insignificant ones, are no longer available, and I am forced to purchase new equipment that I am not familiar with, and put out money I wasn't planning on spending. When did the repair shops for our appliances or replacement parts for same run out of style? I would appreciate an update because I don't remember. And I know I wasn't sleeping for twenty-years, like the legendary Rip Van Winkle I noted earlier in this chapter.

Take for instance our trusty cassette player and the elaborate collection of "our" favorite music from the past—stored on diskettes—

that can't be played on any other machine. Or the VCR, which took some time to master before we could put it to use and enjoy popular movies in the comfort of our home. Both are now considered obsolete and irreplaceable. The CD player replaced the cassettes, and the DVD machine replaced the VCR. But for how long, we are not privy to know. Very disheartening! And it is at those times that I question why is everything changing so rapidly? And I even dare to wish I could turn back the clock to simpler and slower yesteryears or "good old days" despite the fact that those long gone years fell short of present-day conveniences, but somehow we managed to get by without them, appreciated and enjoyed what we did have, and didn't crave for more. Similarly, things didn't seem to wear out as quickly as they do today, or become obsolete before our very eyes. In days passed, household goods usually outlived people and not the other way around.

What happened to the days when a handshake served as a contract between the two parties; when credit at the neighborhood grocery store or a local department store was always good; when charging purchases on credit cards was unheard of; when unpaid bills in the neighborhood stores, were recorded on brown sandwich bags and filed alphabetically under the counter; when bills were always paid on time and the local merchants were never deliberately shortchanged, to my knowledge. And yet, we survived and lived to tell stories about those "good old days"—even though, in reality, they were not always so great, but people who lived through them (and I am one of them) like to think of them in those terms for reasons known to the individual person, alone.

I realize we can't stop progress, but must we hurry through life as we seem to be doing these days, and—to a degree—forced to buy new equipment or household appliances, because new fashions are now the fad, replacement parts for older fixtures no longer available, and repair shops out of style? I miss the days when Sunday was a day to give thanks to God for His blessings, for much needed rest, and for visiting with families and friends. When families took to the parks for relaxing walks, or just resting and reflecting, and even sleep under a shady tree in the park in order to regenerate for the workweek ahead. Unlike today, Sunday is just another busy day of work to catch up on things left undone during the hectic week of work. And one would think with all this—"beyond imagination"—technology, we would have more free time. Am I missing something here, or simply just out of touch with today's way of life? I detest talking to machines when I need a human to talk to regarding something only a person can help me with. I pray the time will never come when people are replaced by robots which are incapable of human feelings and emotions. God help us if this should become a reality!

And what about all those credit cards—I mentioned above—that have invaded our lives today, and make it so easy for us to go beyond and above what we can afford to buy, and get so many of us into deep financial pits? I don't deny the convenience of having them in our wallets, but this "convenience" comes with a heavy price. Using credit cards indiscriminately and being careless about their safety is asking for serious trouble. Keep credit cards on your person at all times! Once—and only once to the best of my recollection—I left my pocketbook in a public place unattended and later found it without my wallet and everything in it missing. Within hours my credit cards were maxed out and my documents in the wallet gone forever, and I worried about identity theft and even purchased special insurance to keep "identity theft" at bay. Where are we going with this? The trouble I went through to replace everything, not counting the missing money, since the credit companies eventually credited my accounts, I pray will never befall anyone I know and don't know as well. This invasion of my privacy happened in April of 2011, but the nightmares of that ill-fated moment continue to haunt me to this day. My heartfelt advice to my readers: Use credit cards only when it's necessary. Pay them in full and on time, and pay cash for everything else. We did that before the introduction of credit cards and it worked. Let's give it another try!

I realize the following segment concerning today's changing weather patterns may not fit "beyond imagination" phenomena, but it is worth noting that our weather is definitely moving in different directions and taking unusual forms. The number of destructive tornadoes and earthquakes that have befallen so many unsuspecting people—not only in our United States but throughout the world—and the unfortunate people who have lost their lives, less important of course, all their possessions. The present-day tornadoes and earthquakes outnumber the ones of the past recorded history. By the same token—to the best of my recollection—winter always remembered to stop by and leave behind mountains of snow in most localities of our state of New Jersey, which remained frozen in most areas, until spring arrived in late March or early April, and on occasions not until early May, but it completely bypassed us in the 2011-2012 winter season. Even Mother Nature seems confused by this strange winter behavior. Flowers and trees came into bloom in February and most were done blooming by the time spring actually arrived. Completely out of character for our area!

It is with a heavy and sorrowful heart that I conclude this "Beyond imagination" chapter. The date was **9/11/2001** and the time around **9:00 AM** when the greatest tragedy in modern history had befallen our beloved nation and affected the whole world. This inconceivable disaster was brought on our unsuspecting country by the ill-spirited, and mentally unbalanced group of terrorists, who conspired against us because they hated us and what we stood for—sweet liberty for all! Three thousand innocent people, and thousands who survived but will never be the same, perished in the New York's renowned Twin Towers' tragedy which forever changed the landscape of one of the greatest cities and financial centers of the world, as well as our empathy for every human being living on this earth. There are despicable individuals on this planet—like the ones who attacked us on 9/11—who are not worthy of anyone's empathy.

We, the people of the United States, will not be surprised by another attack on our country. We know who you are and the grievance you have inflicted on each of us, and all freedom-loving people living on "our" planet Earth. Know that you will be hunted down and brought to justice. Our—fair and just—justice! Many of you already have, including the mastermind of this tragedy, your planner and leader, Osama Bin Laden, who paid for his crimes against humanity with his life.

Freedom Towers—One World Trade Center—now proudly stands in place where the Twin Towers once stood and the structures are the highest skyscrapers in New York City, edging higher than much acclaimed and looked up to Empire State Building. We will never forget the heroes of 9/11 and will forever keep them—and their loved ones—in our hearts and prayers, and see to it that similar tragedy will never befall our beloved country again. That's one promise we, One Nation Under God indivisible, intend to keep. So help us God!

# Chapter Seventeen
## Forever Gifts

No amount of gold, silver, or precious stones, could have brought us as much joy as becoming parents to our two cherished daughters in the first five years of our marriage. And, years later, becoming grandparents to our dearly beloved grandchildren—jointly our "forever gifts" from God. The first grandchild to come into the family was our precious grandson, Adam (his maternal grandfather had the honor of choosing his name), born to our older daughter, Kyra, and her husband, Christopher, residing in Canada. One-and-a-half years later, they welcomed another adorable baby boy to the family and named him Christopher, after his father. Except for the distance between us, which threatened to limit our spontaneous visits to see our growing family beyond the US borders, we were elated on claiming the "rite of passage" into the circles of grandparenthood, and Laura to a proud aunt to her two nephews and also godmother to Adam.

Four plus years had passed since Kyra moved to Montreal to start her married life with her new Canadian (naturalized) citizen husband, Chris, and yet, she never fully adjusted to life outside the "good old" USA—her one and only home until her marriage. Her frequent telephone calls home could not hide the longing she held inside for family and friends she left behind in her native country. We visited as often as was possible with all three of us working. And even met halfway between our respective homes, just to spend some quality time together, especially with our grandsons who were growing by leaps and bounds not only physically but emotionally as well. But seeing them leave in opposite direction from us at the end of our halfway visits was always very painful and tearful. Adam, a toddler now, would hold on to his grandpa with all his might, unwilling to let go, his cries—joined by his baby brother Christopher's—echoing in our minds long after we said our good-byes, was an unsettling feeling that traveled with us all the way home and lasted for days afterwards. Adam was now old enough to express his love, especially for his adoring grandpa, and he didn't hesitate to show it and let you know, in his own innocent babyish way, how he felt.

We were still sleeping when the phone rang one early morning. It was Kyra on the other side of the telephone, tripping over her words. "Mom, I need a favor from you. Christopher left for his business, the babysitter is still not here and I need to jump in the shower before leaving for work. Talk to Adam—keep him busy so he doesn't get himself into trouble without supervision. And don't worry about baby Christopher, he is fast asleep in his crib."

Without further ado—still not fully awake—I was left with toddler Adam on the phone wondering what to say that would keep my two-and-a-half-year-old grandson interested enough to keep on listening for as long as was necessary. But all I could think of at this early hour of the morning was to ask him what he was doing. And I must have asked the same question over and over again. Seemingly annoyed by the repetition, he interrupted my boring spiel, "What do you think I am doing 'g-a-m-a?' I am talking to you, wasting my time when I could be watching 'Power Rangers.'" He managed to say everything in one breath and loud enough so I heard his grievance, before continuing. "G-a-m-a, I don't want to talk to you anymore. I want to talk to g-a-m-pa, so put him on." I was about to wake up his grandpa, when the babysitter must have walked in, because toddler Adam's short attention span turned to Eva, the babysitter, and away from his sleeping grandpa hundreds of miles away and, of course, his boring grandma. Now fully awake, I smiled to myself and wished I was there to squeeze Adam in my arms and tell him how proud I was of him for speaking up for himself, and then take a peek at his baby brother in the crib to make sure he was fully covered and his pacifier was within his reach. Imagine how different our world would be if adults could express their true feelings—as well as truth—as freely as little children do and not worry about the consequences.

"There is hope in our future, says the Lord, that your children shall come back to their own border." Jeremiah 31:17 (NKJV). Imagine my amazement when my eyes fell on this divinely inspired Bible verse when, completely dispirited, I opened a randomly picked up book from the nightstand by the bed, following my telephone conversation with our dejected daughter so far away, and I couldn't be there to cheer her up and help her out. I believed then and still do today, this was a divine message meant especially for me and our family. Within months, Kyra and her family returned to "their own border" and God's unfailing promise was fulfilled.

"Mom, I have some extraordinary news for you that will make you smile. We're coming back to the States! Sit down and I'll tell you all about it so you can share it with daddy and Laura," Kyra excitedly spewed! I couldn't grasp everything all at once, but I wasn't even paying attention to the details. All I heard was that our son-in-law's jewelry business seemed to be spiraling downward, and his partner and he decided to sell the business and move in different directions—his partner with his family to Toronto, and our family, of course, back to the States, close to us. Everything was falling in place according to God's plan. After many years as an educator, John—along with other old timers in the school system—was offered a buyout he couldn't refuse and chose the retirement. His declining health also contributed to the final decision. The company I worked for changed hands, and I chose retirement as well, rather than reemployment with the prevailing company and long distance travel. Everything was timed so perfectly, because *He* willed it so!

Our family was back home in time to celebrate Adam's third birthday in August. His Aunt Laura ordered him a huge decorated birthday cake and we invited a few neighbors with children to help us celebrate. Adam's reaction to the cake and the colorful decorations for this special occasion in our backyard was: "This is the biggest pancake I have ever seen!" referring to the cake and thinking of the famous Polish apple pancakes his daddy was famous for making. Baby Christopher, now one-and-a-half years old, stuck his little finger in the icing on the cake, licked it, and waddled to the miniature playground in our enclosed backyard, compliments of the little ones' overjoyed grandparents. There was enough room in our home for our two families and then some....

Six months later Kyra and Chris and the boys, moved to a home of their own about a half hour from us—by car—in another town, where adorable Christopher celebrated his third birthday. Donned in a black jacket, white shirt, and a bowtie, he slowly walked down the stairs and, when he saw a pile of colorfully wrapped packages and a roomful of people, he stepped in the middle of the room, extended his hands and arms, and with a big smile, greeted all the guests with "Merry Christmas to everybody!" which brought smiles to "everybody." You see, Christmas was long gone, this was January 25th, and little Christopher's third birthday,

Eventually, our son-in-law's mother, Alina Michalski, came from Poland and we shared the caring for our mutual grandsons, because their parents were both working. Those were enchanting years for all of us. Our times together with the boys were filled with new things to explore, games to play, playgrounds to visit, lunches in favorite eateries, picnics and nature walks at the Watchung Mountains, trips to museums, and summer outings to nearby Ocean Grove or to our community pools. We were never lonely, bored, or lacked kisses and hugs. We were blessed! And then—by the grace of God—we were blessed twice more. Now we had four "forever gifts!" Our cup of life's riches was filled to the brim!

Our younger daughter, Laura, and son-in-law, Jonathan, became the proud parents of a beautiful baby girl they lovingly named Kara. Four years later, another precious baby girl joined the overjoyed Dobias family and was appropriately named Faith. The difference our precious granddaughters made in our lives—literally—defies suitable description. I know John joins me when I blatantly declare: We can't even imagine life without them, and we are grateful to God we don't have to. They have blessed our lives with insurmountable joy through the years. Those memorable preschool days we were privileged to experience with them, joyfully shared with their paternal grandparents, Matty and Joe Dobias. The memories we made while babysitting for them will forever remain written in indelible ink in our minds. Who could forget the joys of dance recitals and those elaborate colorful costumes, soccer games, school plays, musical and choral performances in school?

I would be remiss if I failed to mention at least two notable anecdotes from the mouths of our "little but wise" granddaughters. On the preschool playground, while we—Kara's grandparents—were waiting for class dismissal, Kara was engaged in a serious conversation with another preschooler. Her little friend was incessantly bragging about her big brother and how special he was. Kara patiently listened but her patience gave out when she was asked if she had a brother. Kara quickly came to her own defense. "No, I don't have a brother but I have the cutest baby sister and Uncle Jimmy who flies planes." She then looked up to the sky and spotted a plane in the distance. "There is my Uncle Jimmy now," she pointed to the flying plane. "And do you have Uncle Jimmy who flies planes?" The conversation between them ended abruptly. Kara's little friend met her match. They each found other playmates, and all was forgotten. Kudos to you Kara! You held your ground and we were so very proud of you.

While waiting for her big sister, Kara, to finish her dance lesson, my six-year-old granddaughter, Faith, and I took a walk around several blocks, admiring the neighborhood flower gardens. Out of the blue, Faith wanted to know how old I was. Jokingly, I told her I was twenty-one. When I realized she believed me, I confessed to the fib. I then asked her to count and when she reached my age, I would stop her. When Faith couldn't count beyond the number seventy, she stomped her foot and declared, "Grandma, I can't believe God made you live so long!" I asked her if she wanted me to die, she promptly responded. "No, no, Grandma. Of course, I don't want you to die. I want you to live forever, but you have to know you are very, very old." Isn't the innocence of a child great? Faith is now ten years old, but I still smile when I think of that memorable moment. We consider ourselves truly blessed to have had so many unforgettable times with all four of our—pride and joy—grandchildren.

————

**A Brief Note Filled with Love to Each of Our Grandchildren**

*Adam*, you are a handsome young man of "just" twenty-three years old, graduate of the prestigious Penn State University, employed by a notable banking conglomerate, your successful future rests in your capable hands and analytical mind, as well as your business and financial savvy. Keep up the good work, your priorities in check, and follow your dreams.

*Christopher*, you are not quite twenty-two years old, handsome and personable, and have already accomplished so much. Now a senior at Penn State University, majoring in business, the next step is a job in your chosen field that will take you as far as you want to go. Your soft giving heart, strong and agile hands are qualities and talents to be admired.

*Kara*, you are fourteen-and-a-half years old and have shown potentials well beyond your years. You are a lovely and talented young lady, an honor student, a dancer, a musician, a budding writer, and a performer. And all these accomplishments at such a young age! You have to be very proud of yourself. We all are!

*Faith*, at ten years of age, you are our youngest grandchild and precious beyond anything else in the world. Forgive me for continuously reminding you to take your sweet time growing up, since I already know your answer: "Grandma, I have to grow up sometime!" Grow and bloom our precious little one and continue gracing our lives—and the world—with your bright smile, great work in school, unwavering love for animal friends, playing your favorite sport of soccer, and as a budding cellist.

————

**Words of Wisdom to Remember**

Follow good examples and be a good example.

You reap what you sow.

Respect others as you would want them to respect you.

Always do your best and know you have done your best.
Moderation in life is the spice of life.
Jealousy and envy are toxic emotions.
True love conquers all and is all.

# Our Grandchildren: Then and Now

*Adam 22*

*L to R: Christopher 3; Adam 5*

*Christopher 20*

*L to R: Kara 10; Adam 18; Faith 5; Christopher 16*

*Kara 15*

*L to R:   Faith 2;  Kara 6*

*Faith 10*

# Chapter Eighteen
# The Seasons of Life

Spring is this joyous season of year when nature awakens from long winter sleep, and the earth springs back to life. It naturally corresponds to our childhood, the time of innocence, wonder, and carefree days we experience but once in a lifetime, and only for a brief while. Too soon, springtime turns to summer, the season of our youth and early adulthood, when preparations for life ahead must begin. In spite of the gradually increasing responsibilities, however, the young adults remain immersed in their youthfulness through nature's rite of passage. They continue to see the sky at its bluest even on the cloudiest of days. Still naive and inexperienced in life's realities, however, they can easily be lured to bogus promises of the world, make decisions on a whim that fall short of the principles they were taught and the foundations prepared for them, upon which to build successful lives. For the young, the early summer of life is the beginning of a crucial season, not only for the individuals themselves, but also for the world that—sooner or later—will be entrusted to them. The seeds of wisdom, "you reap what you sow," will bring forth many bountiful harvests in autumn, if planted in the fertile fibers of the minds of our young when the season of growth is at its peak.

Winter season is comprised of those senior days known as the "golden years" everyone hopes and expects to attain and enjoy, but the natural progression of life is not all inclusive, and all four seasons of life are not allotted to everybody. One size does not fit all in this case. We are all born at different times, and our days on earth are measured by different factors too. One fact of life we cannot dispute! What many of us seniors—who have reached the ripe old age—can dispute, however, is the presumption that those latter years of our lives are "golden" for all. The majority of us seniors spend our dwindling days visiting doctors, picking up prescriptions, paying house bills—that is, if we're fortunate enough to continue living in our homes and not in senior facilities, including nursing homes; worrying about our fixed incomes, and who's going to take care of us when we're no longer able to take care of ourselves because of debilitating age-related illnesses, advancing years very often bring. This brings me to my own life with my husband, John, our senior years together and, subsequently, by myself.

From my experience today, life is best lived when we take one day at a time, live in the moment, and doing what's best for that specific moment. Plan for tomorrow, but don't worry about tomorrow because—in reality—we only have today. Unfortunately, that's easier said than done and I can attest to that. I am a chronic worrier and have been as far back as I can remember. And did my worry change the outcome of things to come and still hidden from me? I think not, but they did contribute—I believe—to my problematic insomnia and myriad of other worry-related health problems that might have been avoided if I let myself relax, take life less seriously, and laughed at myself more. By the same token, it wasn't my constant worry about my husband's declining health, beginning at age fifty. It was timely medical—and divine—intervention that, blessedly, granted him twenty-six additional years with us after the first unfavorable diagnosis. When arteriosclerosis (blockages in his arteries) were detected, angioplasties—by a cardiologist in the hospital setting—were performed, followed by multiple stent-implants at later dates, which kept the blocked arteries open for sufficient blood flow to the heart. When less invasive medical procedures on his ailing knees stopped working, his left knee was replaced twice, which meant long rehabilitation in those early days. And when cancer was found in his kidney, we had the cancerous kidney removed. His final battle with cancer began and ended with prostate cancer which—undetected in time even under controlled situation—metastasized to his bones, and eventually to the rest of his body, in spite of every medical effort to reverse its progression once discovered two years earlier. In every case, it wasn't my excessive worry that prolonged his life, it was vigilance and action.

My beloved husband of forty-eight years, father of two loving daughters, and grandfather of four adoring grandchildren, took his last breath on October 4, 2010 at the age of seventy-six—two years shy of our fiftieth wedding anniversary, and was put to rest—as fate would have—on the day of our forty-eighth wedding anniversary. Except for the last three days in the hospital in a coma with family by his side, continuously holding his hand, I was taking care of him at home, with the assistance of our two caring daughters, and help from the dedicated hospice people, whose support at that crucial time in our lives meant the world to us and will never be forgotten.

I should have known my dear husband's long-suffering days were nearing the end when, on two occasions, he grabbed my hands, kissed them tenderly, and tearfully thanked me for taking such good care of him, and for the forty-eight years of our marriage as well. He knew his days on earth were numbered, but the merciful God kept that truth away from me and, instead, blessed me with strength to do what needed to be done, keep my focus on the moment and not the reality of tomorrow over which I had no control. It was hope and faith that sustained me through those difficult times, and strength from Above to keep the vigil burning for both of us to the end.

———

### Out of My Sight but Not Out of My Heart

The day of the funeral was shrouded in sadness and confusion. The family and friends stood by me throughout this trying time, but at the end of all the formalities, everyone went their way and, except for the brief time with my immediate family at home, I would be left by myself. They, too, had to leave. The grandchildren had to go back to school the next day and our daughters and their spouses, back to work. How will I fare the first night in the house alone? On the surface, I tried to be brave and assured my family I would be okay, but on the inside I wasn't as sure—the feeling I wanted to keep to myself. My daughters helped me find an appropriate place to display the American flag I proudly received at the gravesite in honor of my husband's service to his country during the Korean conflict, hugged me good-bye and one by one went their ways, as I wanted them to do, for their sakes. I regretted my decision to stay in the house by myself that first night as soon as the short October day turned to all darkness, and crushing, painful reality took over. My husband was never coming back, and I was now a widow—the word I dreaded with every fiber of my being.

I sat in my husband's favorite recliner, pressed his picture to my heart, closed my eyes, and—in the quietude of the moment—tried to envision us as parents of young kids again, frolicking in the roaring ocean waves on hot summer days at the Jersey Shore, hoping the memories of those cherished moments would replace the gloomy thoughts of reality squeezing every last bit of life from my already withered spirit—at least for that first night at home by myself. And as hard as I tried to push those painful thoughts out of my overburdened mind, they only seemed to multiply. Even the old grandfather clock that's been in our family for years stopped cooperating. It kept on chiming louder than it ever did before, which made the house sound hollow and appear depressed, not cheerful like in the past. The dismal thoughts persisted until they reached a boiling point—a point of no return. And then the realization that our time as husband and wife and as a family under one roof was never to be again, and I must travel the rest of this journey called life alone. The word "alone" was enough to literally freak me out. The grandfather clock chimed ten times when I made a decision to take action. The light in the friendly neighbor's house—directly across from our house—was, thankfully, still on. I dialed their number and asked if I could spend the night with them. In their peaceful guest room, I quickly fell into a—much needed—restful, deep sleep. At the first sign of daybreak, I jumped out of bed, walked to the window facing our house and—still dazed by the events of the last few days—transfixed, tried to put things into some kind of perspective that would make sense to me and I could handle.

The early morning mist was hovering over the house, and the tree on the front lawn seemed half-empty of "yesterday's" vibrant greenery, which made our once happy home appear forlorn and abandoned, and caused me to feel guilty for even harboring the thoughts of walking away from it, and seek other alternatives for my life as our concerned daughters had suggested. In time, my doubts if I could live in the house by myself disappeared like darkness at sunrise of that first night. I realized it won't be easy to embark on this new journey in my later years, but I would give it my very best, including the heart our house now needed to make it a loving home again, not only for me, but also for the family and friends who would be most welcomed. A home reminiscent of the past! I left a thank you note on the kind neighbors' dining room table and crossed the street to my own safe harbor. The morning fog was lifting and the sun was breaking through the clouds when I opened the gate to our backyard and noticed a few ripened tomatoes still clinging to the mother vines, and one huge, red tomato in the middle of the picnic table—its presence there unbeknownst—welcoming me home.

The first few days living alone in the house were shrouded in loneliness and grief beyond anything I lived through before. Everything I touched reminded me of my dear husband and faithful friend of forty-eight years. Simple things like one-plate setting on the table and a single toothbrush in the toothbrush holder would bring me to tears. No, our life was not perfect, but whose life really is? We argued, disagreed, and stubbornly stood our ground on issues that concerned us individually, but we never walked out on each other. That was never an option. Our commitment to each other was stronger than any argument or disagreement could ever be. And our love, faith, and trust in God and each other transcended any—and all—lows of life everyone experiences, sooner or later. How well I remember discussions that lasted till the wee hours of the morning, when we couldn't resolve our differences in a timely manner, or before we kissed good night which, at times, was not until early morning. I credit our successful marriage to good communication, compromise, at times giving in for the sake of peace, and not always expecting 50% contribution from each other, because that would be unreasonable and unfair.

We mourned together and comforted each other when our parents passed from this life to the next. When our siblings left this world much too soon—my brother Michael at age fifty-five, and John's sister, Anna, in her late fifties. The most recent passing of our nephew, Charles Michael (Anna's and Charles Csernica's son) at age fifty; my sister-in-law (my brother Michael's wife) Justina Czerhoniak in her early eighties; and my faithful, longtime friend, Lilian Kopetz, in her seventies. And on February 14, 2013, my sister-in-law, Eva Fedash—John's sister—succumbed to pancreatic cancer at age eighty-two. And so many, many good friends that left big voids in our hearts. To each and all—including my beloved husband and my dear brother John, who fell asleep in the Lord on October 4, 2013 of Alzheimer's disease at age 86. I pray that you are at peace and preparing a place for us when our time on earth is no more, which is everybody's eventual destiny. I believe, with my whole heart and soul, that we will see each other again. For the time being, we must remain physically separated but, spiritually, we are still together, because love is eternal and ever binding.

My husband John remains such a big part of my life, his presence continues to reflect in my nightly dreams and he is as real as ever. The days are always sunny when I am with him, either at the shore or in the mountains, holding hands like always, enjoying our time together. In my dreams, I know that he has passed on, but the reality of the moment makes me question the fact, and I hear myself saying: "People say that you died, but you really didn't. Let's keep this a secret between the two of us!" He smiles, and I wake up—sadly much too soon and empty-handed. Similarly, during the last hours in the hospital, our daughters insisted that I get some much needed rest at our younger daughter and son-in-law Jonathan's home, only minutes down the road from the hospital. Reluctantly, I agreed. Laura dropped me off and rushed back to the hospital to be near her dying father and sister, Kyra, keeping vigil.

It must have been after midnight when I walked in. To my utter surprise, the music of our favorite classic we used to dance to on our wedding anniversaries—a tradition of ours—"Autumn Leaves" by Roger Williams, resonated from every corner of the house. After a while, I asked my son-in-law, Jonathan, to please either lower the music or take it off altogether, only to be told there was no music playing. In fact that particular oldie was not even in their music collection. I rested my feet for a few minutes, called Laura in the hospital and urged her to come for me, immediately. I made it in time to grab my husband's dying hand and whisper in his ear. "Our forty-eighth wedding anniversary is almost here. They're playing our song, "Autumn Leaves." He mustered enough strength to squeeze my hand and tears rolled down his face. He heard the music too! And some still say there is no such thing as a bridge connecting this world with the next?

# Chapter Nineteen
## Moving On....

**"Stopping by Woods on a Snowy Evening"**
**by my favorite poet, Robert Frost**

*"The woods are lovely, dark and deep,*
*But I have promises to keep,*
*And miles to go before I sleep,*
*And miles to go before I sleep."*

I chose the last stanza of the above epic poem as the motto to live by when giving up would have been easier than "moving on" during those difficult first days, weeks, and months alone. When fear of facing the future without the support of my devoted husband barraged my mind with more fear. "Fear," that—more often than not—immobilized my spirit from moving forward, and I found myself aimlessly pacing the floor from room to room, painfully reliving the last days, hours, and minutes in the hospital room next to my dying husband, and then those somber days that followed, which brought me to this irrevocable moment. And now, as a widow, much like a ship on a turbulent ocean, without a captain at the helm. I prayed for courage to brave the uncharted waters before me, and resilience to stay afloat until the waves of gripping grief carried me to calmer waters, and eventually to the peaceful shore where I would find solace and inspiration to go on. And I believe with all my heart and soul, God answered my prayers because He comforted me, blessed me with hope, and gave me strength to pull myself out of the abyss of grief which was suffocating my spirit.

I heard people say to the bereaved that "time heals all wounds." My experience with grief and its relation to time takes a different view. Time only hardens the skin over a grievous wound, which makes it less painful for the bereft to move forward, but underneath the callused skin, the wound remains time-defiant. Grief changes us and the way we look at life, even if the bereaved believes, as I do, that the separation from the loved one is only physical and temporary. The fact still remains—the earthly loss is permanent and irreversible, and we must learn to live with this daunting reality if we want to move on as we should and must, for the peace of our departed loved ones, and for ourselves to continue living a productive life.

Truly, when God closes the doors, He always leaves a window open somewhere in the house. I found that open window when I uncovered several written chapters of *Those Fleeting Years*—a sequel to my *Blossoms on a Rooftop*—I had put on the side, and eventually out of mind two plus years earlier, when my priority became my husband's care. Holding the unfinished manuscript in my hands and flipping through the completed pages enlivened my spirit and brought new meaning to my empty life. The reality that John read, and re-read, the finished chapters and left his heartprints of approval on each, made this our project and story, and it was now up to me to bring this narrative of our married life to completion and fruition—my saving grace and inspiration to begin "moving on" because I still had "miles to go before I sleep," metaphorically speaking.

There were so many tasks awaiting my attention, in addition to my unfinished manuscript. There were bills to be paid, documents to be processed, such as social security, insurances, transfer of properties, telephone calls to be made, memorial gifts to be acknowledged.... And there was my brother, John—seven years my senior, unmarried and childless—in advance stages of Alzheimer's disease. As the power of attorney for his estate and an only surviving sibling, I felt obliged—

and legally responsible—for his care. I hired a live-in caregiver. It was his wish to stay in his home in Jersey City, about twenty-five miles from my home in Cranford, so I visited regularly to check on things, even though my brother no longer knew me. There was more work to do than hours in the day, but my unfinished manuscript kept me grounded, inspired, and close to my husband, John, and busy enough for both of us. The decisions—and work—we did together, now rested on my shoulders alone. I didn't realize how much work my caring husband did on the outside of the house and on the inside to keep everything running smoothly, until I had to do it all myself or hire someone to do it for me. There is much more to owning a home, I soon realized, than dusting the furniture, vacuuming the carpets and floors, putting meals on the table, changing the bed and curtains—in all due respect for the homemaker—which was my contribution to household chores, when we worked as a team. How unfortunate that, in a busy life, we sometimes take each other for granted and don't realize it until it is too late. Closely intertwined lives may account for this inadvertent blunder.

In addition to intense grief and shock that come with losing a loved one, burdensome thoughts of "what if" moments also need to be reckoned with, processed and put to rest in the steps to healing. What if we had done "this or that," would my husband's life have been saved or prolonged? What if we had changed doctors and hospital and taken John out of state for unconventional treatment, would he still be alive today? On and on...since we can't bring our loved one back. How strange that we seem to concentrate on things that were not done for our departed loved one, rather than on things that were done, such as loving care and latest treatments. This phenomenon is known as "false guilt"—I learned about later—most of us experience when losing a loved one, since there is nothing more we can do for them, so we boggle our minds with things that were not done, even if we were not aware of their existence at the time.

When spring came, I planted flowers around the house like in the past when we gardened together, prepared Easter dinner for the family, filled plastic colored eggs with candy along with money, and scattered them throughout the greening backyard—in inconspicuous places—for the grandchildren to find. A tradition we perpetuated throughout the years, going back to the time when our daughters believed in Easter Bunny, and heard Santa atop the snowy rooftop, spurring his reindeer on Christmas Eve. This first Easter celebration without my husband was reminiscent of other Easters in our home, but the mood reflected the undeniable reality of the moment. The veil of sadness was miraculously lifted from our somber faces when our two young granddaughters, Kara and Faith, brought in baskets full of Easter eggs from the backyard, dumped them in the middle of the living room floor, and gleefully began counting their coins to see who got more, while popping chocolate Easter Bunnies and marshmallow chicks into their mouths. Oh, the joy of God's children! Their innocence was reason enough to laugh again—and we did.

Our day-trips to the country to see nature in bloom in spring, the Jersey Shore in summertime to watch the ocean waves wash upon the shore, or drives to nearby mountains in the fall to see the colorful foliage were special times we both enjoyed immensely. Those cherished days were gone, and to decry the fate would not change the present without a new beginning.

These days, weather permitting, you will find me reading a book on a park bench in Cranford's Nomahegan Park, enhanced by a lake and cherry trees that create a spectacle of beauty every spring. You will see me walking on the sidewalks of our quaint town, looking at window displays, or having a relaxing lunch in one of town's familiar eateries where people know me and take time to ask how I am doing. You can spot me on the banks of the Cranford's Rahway River, enjoying the peaceful waters flowing by leisurely to another destination.

Being blessed with grandchildren, I automatically became a grandma not only to my children's children, but also to their pets. On two separate occasions in the summer of 2012, two of my four-legged granddaughters—one Kyra's and the other one Laura's—stayed with me while their families were on vacations. Lo and behold, I became bonded with them and enjoyed having them with me. In the past, I dreaded coming to an empty house, now there was a kitty greeting me at the door and happy to see me. When my furry granddaughters were picked up by their rightful owners, I missed their cheery company and unconditional love. That got me thinking. Why not a kitty of my own? And I adopted a one-and-a-half-year-old handsome, orange with white trim male kitty, and named him Sunny because he makes my days sunny even if the sun is hiding behind the clouds. Thank you all encompassing Heavenly Father for showing me the way!

# More Family Pictures

*Bride's family - My brother Michael's Family's first Christmas in America (1960): Back row L to R: Nephew Roman; brother Michael and sister-in-law Justina; Bottom Row L to R: Nieces: Luba, Myra & Eugenia.*

*L to R: 1 yr old Laura on her daddy's lap, and 4 yr old Kyra on her mommy's lap*

*L to R: Kyra 7 and Laura 4 in matching dresses made by me*

*Luba and John's 40th Wedding Anniversary*

*Left to right: Christopher 18; Adam 20; Daughter Kyra and son-in-law Christopher.*

*Left to right: Kara 15; son-in-law Jonathan, Daughter Laura and Faith 10 years old.*

*Our one and only "Home Sweet Home".*

*My new furry friend "Sunny"*

# Chapter Twenty
## Lessons Life Has Taught Me

"We get too soon oldt undt too late schmart." The origin of the fore-going proverb mentioned elsewhere in this book, as well, is credited to the Pennsylvania Dutch people of the early twentieth century (circa 1920s). A deep-rooted, timeless belief that still reverberates today in the year 2013, close to one hundred years later. Those of us who have traveled the full circle of life's highway can best attest to the validity of this ageless fact, and since I count myself among them, I, too, can attest to this fundamental truth. We "do" get too soon old and too late smart, because wisdom comes from longevity of living, dealing with stumbling blocks along the way, and learning how to avoid them in the future. A feat for which duration of time is necessary to realize the gift of fruition, which is wisdom.

Growing up, I thought life was forever and so was my youthful-ness, and old age belonged to people who were already old. Was this erroneous perception stemming from having spent most of my early childhood years tending cattle in the pasture fields, all alone—and not learning the fundamentals of life in school—when one single day seemed to last forever and there seemed to be no end to them? From my vantage point today, I am amazed how quickly those precious years have flown by, and stealthily changed me—literally—from my head to my toes.

My light brown hair is now silver-gray; my bifocals are my steady company; gravity has taken back almost two inches of my height; and the quick sprint in my walk has been reduced to calculated steps. But I am not complaining and have no regrets. The silver in my hair and smaller frame serve as testaments to ageless spirit, especially in tough times; the bifocals are in defiance of my aging vision; the slower pace to get me where I need to go safely and unhurriedly, while enjoying the displays of nature's changing seasons along the way. The expression "the only constant in life is change" is worthy of acceptance, because—truly—that's what life is all about, constant change.

It's refreshing to know we don't just wake up one morning, look in the mirror, and see a reflection of an old person staring back. If this was my youthful perception of old age—and I believe it was—no wonder the thought of it left me breathless with fear and apprehension. Time has shown me that our journey to the place of "old" is gradual, subtle, and natural and does not change who we are on the inside—the essence of our spirit that lives on.

Life has also taught me that age is relative! I remember my mother's fiftieth birthday when I was still in my early twenties. I panicked and lost a whole night's restful sleep because I honestly thought my dear mother was very old and would soon die. And she looked aged too, not only because of her fragile health, but also because of the way she dressed—dress code mature women were expected to conform to, such as tight hair perms, or straight hair severely pushed back and twisted into a bun, long shapeless dresses, and stubby-heeled, black laced leather shoes, which minimized their statures and made them appear much older than their age. Times have changed and so have our mindsets concerning aging. Today's women shop for fashionable clothes that compliment their bodies, and not age-appropriate garb their predecessors observed; visit beauty salons almost as often as their much younger counterparts do; and, unlike their mothers and grandmothers, they don't wear aprons around the house. Have you noticed this evolution? I have, because I identify myself with it. In my updated view regarding aging, age fifty is simply a start of a new

chapter in life to be embraced joyfully, barring, of course, any unfore-
seen eventualities that might have altered this natural progression of
life. And now to the next lesson life has taught me.

Being truthful is the best, safest, and easiest way to live,
because you don't have to remember what story you've told and to
how many people, should retraction of same become necessary.
Guilty as charged to some deliberate fibs I've told in my much
younger days, lived to regret them in each case, and took the lessons
I had learned from my blunders to heart. This is not to say that an
occasional truth is best kept to oneself. Take for instance the following anecdote, cute because it was spilled by an innocent child of
six, my precious granddaughter, Faith.

I was delighted to see Faith holding the beautifully embroidered—in my opinion—denim handbag I had given to her mother,
my daughter, Laura, for a present the previous Christmas, and had
not seen it in use until this moment. Faith was obediently standing
in front of the restroom following her dance recital, waiting for her
mommy to come out, pressing the oversized bag to her chest which
I recognized at first glance.

"I am glad to see you taking such good care of your mother's
handbag," I said to my granddaughter. Her unabated response stunned
me with surprise and I was lost for words.

"No, Grandma. This is my bag now! Mommy gave it to me to
carry my stuffed animals when we're away from home, because that's
the only thing this bag is good for, she said." Faith firmly stated,
looked up and—without second-guessing herself—sputtered.
"Grandma, why did you buy such an ugly handbag for my mommy?"
And, as if that wasn't enough to carry the message home, she added,
"Mommy hates it!"

I will forever treasure this unforgettable moment, and a myriad of
other such moments with my children and grandchildren. Truth may
hurt but it drives the message home. Faith is now a young lady of
eleven, and knows that some things are better off left unsaid. Oh! how
I miss that precious stage of her childhood when she said—as little
children do—what she thought about things from her own innocent
perspective, and didn't hold anything back for fear of repercussion,
because this complex word was not yet in her vocabulary, just as set-

ting boundaries was missing from mine, until I finally found it in my later years.

The spirit of invincibility belongs to the young, but those magical years, like everything else in life—good or bad—don't last forever. Sooner for some and later for others, there comes a time when being "everything to everybody" is no longer possible, and setting new boundaries for self-preservation becomes necessary. For me, this moment became real sometime in my early sixties, when my youthful strength was noticeably waning, and I could no longer be that "some-one" everybody could count on for everything. It took several unsuc-cessful tries before I felt comfortable saying "no" without feeling guilty, and profusely apologizing for the disappointment I might have caused someone. The expression "you must first save yourself before you can save others" saved me from virtually stretching the rubber band of life beyond its strength.

I would be remiss if I failed to share several other valuable lessons I took from my life experiences: Procrastination creates needless stress with dire consequences in the long run. Doing what one can do today, will leave tomorrow for new adventures and free the mind of unnecessary worries that may lead to ill health. By the same token, making promises that cannot be fulfilled from the get go will promote distrust and hard feelings in relationships and ruin friendships. It's bet-ter to follow the rule of thumb which is "say what you mean, and mean what you say." For the same reason, stay away from degrading words regarding others. Demeaning words can be powerful weapons that can result in permanent damage to other's spirit and confidence. I relate to such obtrusive behavior by several insensitive individuals who have crossed my path in the past, and I concur with our much admired for-mer first lady, humanitarian, and writer, Mrs. Eleanor Roosevelt (1884-1962), who—relating to her own life—once said: "I can forgive but how do I forget?" Verbal assault can result in trauma capable of rooting itself into one's mind and—overtime—assume a life of its own in defiance of eradication. There is no sound reason for using hurtful words when kinder ones can deliver the same message!

My confidence grew along with my age. I am no longer shy about asking questions for fear they may be dumb, or speak my mind for fear I may sound foolish. Time has taught me that questions deserve answers—none are dumb—and minds deserve freedom of expression—and none are foolish. I learned from years of experience that being a good listener—and less of a talker—is the greatest gift one can give to a friend or a loved one. But there is a catch to this scenario. True friends are few and far in between, and we must choose wisely. We can choose our friends but not our family!

**A thought to my younger readers:** The last thing young people think about is putting a portion of their earnings away for the future, because the "future" seems so far away, and the present is brimming with enticement for spending every penny earned. I know, I've been there, believe it or not! And if it wasn't for one special friend in the company I worked for—many years my senior—who took time to set me on the right financial path from the get go, I might be chastising myself today for bypassing this golden opportunity when saving through payroll deduction, matched by the employer was easy and hardly made a dent in my take-home pay, but of such financial comfort in my retirement years. Ann was my blessing in my youth! May I be in yours? And let me—if I may—leave this thought with you regarding finances: It's not how much money you make, it's what you do with it! Invest some of it wisely.

I am a firm believer that miracles do happen, and some clouds come with silver linings. Let me exemplify this belief. The super storm "Irene" of 2011 devastated our township of Cranford with incredible floods, which personally affected me as well. With loss of power for many days, the two electric sump pumps in the half-completed basement, where most of our valuables were kept, stopped working in time, creating a cesspool in the basement, our irreplaceable possessions submerged in it. When the rains finally stopped and the water from the basement pumped out, the heartbreaking task of cleaning up—moving everything from the basement to the curb—had begun. My thoughts of sadness for all the treasured memories lost in the flood were interrupted by my daughter, Laura, who was helping with the cleanup, calling out to me.

"Mom, an envelope addressed to you fell out of Daddy's grammar school dictionary," the one book from the past, my husband kept and treasured for all these years, because it reminded him of his childhood. "Do you want it?" she questioned. I reached for the envelope, but seeing how very wet it was, decided to dry it on the sunny backyard patio first before finding what was hiding inside this mystery letter-size envelope, decorated with artsy hearts on the outside. When it dried enough, I carefully lifted the unsealed envelope flap and peeked in. A card enhanced by more hearts came into view. My curiosity piqued, I yanked the card from the envelope! Lo and behold, enclosed in the card was a handwritten letter edged with more artfully fashioned hearts—art and handwriting I instantly recognized as unmistakably my husband's, who had passed on one year earlier.

My hands shaking and tears trickling down my cheeks, I began reading this unexpected treasured letter, which read in part, much more of personal nature left out:

> *"You will always be my Love,*
> *My Life, My all.*
> *You are as beautiful to me today*
> *As you were 47 years ago.*
> *Physically we have changed,*
> *But spiritually no.*
> *I will love you throughout eternity.*
> *Thank you for everything!"*

It's uncanny how the "storm" that destroyed my—temporary—earthly memories turned out to be the catalyst for the forever memory from beyond I fervently believe. I keep this unforgettable last testimony to our love under my pillow and read it often, because it brings me comfort knowing that true love transcends time and space, as well as physical death. And here is another testament in support of miracles:

Among the most treasured artifacts destroyed in the flood Irene were my late husband's unfinished religious icons—images of saints, referred to as writing of icons, not painting—used in the devotions of Eastern Christians' churches and homes. Due to the nature of John's labor of love, we decided to store the water-logged, lopsided icons in safe place, identify the contents, and not expecting to open the cardboard boxes anytime soon—if ever. But that's not how miracles work, it was soon reaffirmed to me. "Thanks to the lovely Maja—an iconographer from Serbia, who recently immigrated to America to marry her long-distance sweetheart, the handsome Michael Rossi, PhD—the awash icons received second chance. The first icon to be restored and finished by Maja was the image of Jesus, my husband's ultimate goal to have completed by our fiftieth wedding anniversary—which would have been a very special occasion unbeknownst to Maja.

The icon of Christ was blessed by Reverend Emil Minkovich, our dedicated pastor, following the liturgy commemorating the second anniversary of my husband's passing, and our unfulfilled fiftieth wedding anniversary—with Maja and Michael in attendance to add to the surprise that brought unexpected sunshine to an otherwise cloudy day for our family. Maja's new mother-in-law, Mrs. Irene Rossi, the choir director, sang the responses as well as John's favorite hymn. Irene's beautiful voice filled the church with goodness on that special day, and promise of God's blessings for tomorrow. Welcome to America and to the Rossi family Maja, and thank you for blessing our family with your God-given talent. You remind me of myself sixty-some years ago, that's probably why I felt such a strong connection to you my young friend the minute we first met. And I know you will be just as successful as I have been—or more—in this "land of the free and unlimited opportunity," because we share similar roots and upbringing. God grant you, Maja and Michael, many blessed years!

In closing this narrative, *Those Fleeting Years,* the sequel to *Blossoms on a Rooftop,* I wish to thank you most sincerely for taking time to read this sequel, and leave you with the following recipe for a happy, fulfilling life mentioned elsewhere in the book, yet worthy of repeating when intended for a blessing:

*Someone to Love*
*Something to Do*
*Something to Look Forward To*

May your life be blessed with all three ingredients, and may you enjoy the fruits of your labor in peace when your life's work is done, happily watching the world go by!

**Corinthians 13:13 (King James 2000 Bible @2003)**
**"Now these three remain: faith, hope, and love.**
**But the greatest of these is LOVE."**

**Paraphrased from**
**"Stopping by Woods on a Snowy Evening**
**by Robert Frost**

*The springtime meadows are lovely and enticing*
*to the weary traveler but I have work to complete before*
*I can sleep!*

# An Addendum to *Those Fleeting Years*
# Expressions Indigenous to American English Language

My fascination with analogous expressions unique to American English language captivated my interest even before my knowledge of the newly acquired English was sufficient enough to meet their challenges. Listed below are some of my favorite practical wisdom phrases I collected over the years and wish to share with you, dear readers:

- You don't get a second chance to make a first impression.

- You can lead a horse to the water but you can't make him drink.

- A penny saved is a penny earned.

- Pennywise and pound foolish.

- Waste not, want not.

- Don't count your chickens before they hatch.

- A bird in hand is worth two in the bush.

- Don't fix something if it's not broken.

- If you play with fire, you're going to get burned.

- If you need something done, ask a busy person.

- Anything worth achieving comes with a struggle.

- Light a candle and don't curse the darkness.

- What good is a dream if you don't share it.

- Don't promise what you can't deliver.

- Gather "ye" roses while you may.

- Perception is reality.

- One person's trash is another's treasure.

- One step at a time is the only way to get you where you want to go.

- An ounce of prevention is worth a pound of cure.

- Where your heart is, that's where your treasure is.

- It's not what you have in life, what matters is what you make of it.

- The night is always darkest before the dawn.

- Patience is a virtue.

- If you don't know (study) history, you're bound to repeat it.

- Don't use all the water on too small a fire.

- Do you want to be right or do you want peace?

- Fool me once, fool me twice, fool me three times and I am the fool.

- Strike when the iron is hot.

*"The Best of Times"*
*Luba and John at their younger daughter's wedding in 1993.*

Treasured paintings depicting
"Seasons" by my late husband
John, artist extraordinaire.